Ceremonial Culture ir

Ceremonial Culture

in

Pre-Modern Europe

edited by

NICHOLAS HOWE

UNIVERSITY OF NOTRE DAME PRESS

NOTRE DAME, INDIANA

Library of Congress Cataloging-in-Publication Data
Ceremonial culture in pre-modern europe / editor, Nicolas Howe.
    p.   cm.
Includes index.
ISBN-13: 978-0-268-03075-9 (pbk. : alk. paper)
ISBN-10: 0-268-03075-8 (pbk. : alk. paper)
1. Europe—Religious life and customs.   2. Europe—Religion.   I. Howe, Nicholas.
BL690.C47   2007
390.094—dc22

                                                    2006032465

Contents

Acknowledgments

My thanks go first to Suzanne Childs and Wendy Matlock who worked with me at the Center for Medieval and Renaissance Studies at the Ohio State University when this volume began its existence. Their dedication and enthusiasm were enormously helpful. I must also thank Barbara Hanrahan of the University of Notre Dame Press for staying with this project over the years and for guiding it from manuscript to volume. I want also to thank the contributors to this volume for their patience and willingness to believe me when I reported that progress was being made.

Introduction

NICHOLAS HOWE

The phrase "ceremonial culture," as used in the title of this volume, pro-
poses that such enactments as processions, dramas, rituals, and liturgies
are sufficiently alike to reward comparative study. There are, from the
start, distinctions to be drawn among them: some are performed in public spaces like streets and squares, others in sacred spaces like churches
and cathedrals; some are meant to legitimate political power, others to
manifest the presence of the sacred on earth; some acquire their power
through the knowledge that they have been repeated, others by being
understood as unique or originary performances. Beyond such differences, these forms display certain common features. Each gives a physical presence to beliefs or ideas that might otherwise escape direct appre-
hension. Each renders the ineffable or spiritual in its own way as visible
or palpable. In the process, each ceremony becomes a visual drama with
highly scripted acts, movements, and rhythms. And each must have a
clear understanding of the expectations shared by its audiences or witnesses, especially if it is to make them complicit in its work. Any instance
of ceremony is, finally, an attempt to close the divide between abstract
and literal, ideal and actual. In all of these ways, processions, dramas, rituals, and liturgies gain their life and power, both as events in their own
time and place and as objects of study for later generations.

As they perform these varieties of cultural work, ceremonies enable the continuity of beliefs and practices across generations as well as their spread into new territories. Such is most evident of liturgies that enact and reenact the spiritual dramas of a religious faith that declares itself eternal and universal. Even royal processions figured around the person of a single monarch at a specific time can exploit ceremony to endure beyond one moment of performance. Such processions typically acquire their authority by imitating earlier processions of a similar type and do so knowingly, even ostentatiously, to assert that a ruler's power will extend into a distant future. Ceremonies are not isolated in their own performance, but instead concentrate past and future into a moment of enactment. The belief or idea they make palpable and visible may thus be demonstrated to be eternal rather than ephemeral, universal rather than local, true rather than false.

Ceremonial culture in the pre-modern world presents a complex set of methodological issues. The types of evidence available to scholars and thus the degree of authority they can bring to their discussion must be considered from the outset. That evidence is by and large drawn from archival materials, extant images, and surviving architectural remains. Cultural anthropologists interested in ceremonies can, in contrast, witness not simply the events themselves but also the ritual preparations for them made within the community. And they can, in turn, track the consequences that follow performance or enactment within that same community. Anthropologists observe from their professional position, but they sometimes move toward becoming participants as they ask questions and gather information that cannot be deduced immediately or easily from the performance of a ceremony. Under certain conditions, they may even see a ceremony repeated or reenacted, and thus can consider if its form is invariable or if it responds to changes in its culture. Perhaps most crucially, observers who are able to witness a ceremony can plot how it uses space, how its participants arrange or disperse themselves, how they move or resist moving from point to point, how they are clothed and otherwise adorned. In other words, such witnesses are able to appreciate the dynamic choreography of a ceremony as it engages with time and place. Anthropologists can, in short, gather the local knowledge that surrounds a ceremony and enables it to be enacted.

Denied the possibility of personal observation, how are scholars to understand ceremonies such as a Catholic liturgical procession that moved through a medieval townscape or the triumphal entry of a Renaissance ruler into a subjected city? If one were studying a past culture without written records, it would be very difficult to articulate these questions, let alone to answer them. But the instances of ceremony I have just evoked belong to cultures that possessed very developed forms of literacy as well as privileged groups charged with the work of writing. A great deal of documentary evidence survives from pre-modern Europe to help us frame the necessary questions about their ceremonies, and it is sometimes accompanied by relevant visual and material evidence. In certain cases, the ceremonial space remains intact at least in part (or can be imaginatively reconstructed) and thus offers some clues about where participants in the ceremony moved and from where observers watched them. Extant ground plans and building facades can also help one reconstruct the ways in which ceremonies were performed and observed.

Yet there is something of a paradox in all of this, or at least a cautionary irony. These ceremonies, which must often be reconstructed from written sources, were intended to do their work and acquire meaning beyond the textual realm. As they exist apart from the textual, ceremonies have obvious utility for those who belong to non-literate societies or for those who live largely outside of written culture in otherwise literate societies. As performative ceremonies, they were meant to be enacted and witnessed. Nor did this witnessing follow the passive, one-way flow through which we experience many of our ceremonies, that is, television broadcasts of spectacles such as the Macy's Thanksgiving Day parade, celebratory rituals of the Olympic Games, political processions such as the anniversary of a revolution or the opening of the British Parliament, or the ritual presentation of military units to commemorate national holidays. Staring at the screen, we can observe the event but those engaged in the spectacle or ceremony cannot look back at those of us who are its designated, if disembodied, spectators. As Michel de Certeau observes in *The Practice of Everyday Life*: "The television viewer cannot write anything on the screen of his set. He has been dislodged from the product; he plays no role in its apparition."[1] Our television viewing of rituals is curiously detached: they have been reduced to mere entertainment and, as such, must compete for our attention with other offerings on television, including advertisements. When that happens, ceremonies become entertainment and thus can be enjoyed or, just as likely, dismissed as boring.

In that sense, they exist at our choice: we can turn off the television and leave the realm of the ceremonial in ways that were less instantaneously possible for witnesses on the narrow streets of an early modern town or in the precincts of a medieval cathedral. Our boredom and detachment when watching televised ceremonies were not, one suspects, frequently felt by those who witnessed and performed in pre-modern ritual ceremonies and dramas precisely because they were present at the scene and perceived it through a full array of their senses. To observe meant to participate. By contrast, only a few family members or friends are likely to know that we participate in a ceremony when we watch it on television within our own private realm.

The studies in the present volume aim at identifying and recovering the excitement and dynamism that characterized ceremonial culture in pre-modern Europe.[2] While each contributor examines the topic of ceremonial culture in ways that correspond to his or her own research interests, each also turns and returns to certain key issues: the relation between public and private space, the development of fully developed dramas and rituals from earlier forms, and the semiotic code that the ceremony in question manifested to its original audience. Throughout these chapters runs another common thread: that these pre-modern ceremonies evolved within a very different world than any we are likely to know today. Indeed, one is tempted to say that these ceremonies are no longer part of our world precisely because they exist as objects of scholarly study rather than as moments of active participation and witnessing.

That pre-modern ceremonies are very different from our own is made abundantly clear by Margot Fassler's "*Adventus* at Chartres: Ritual Models for Major Processions." As we visit Chartres today, we see a great cathedral set in the midst of a prosperous provincial town. The postcard shops and restaurants surrounding the cathedral remind us that today most visitors observe a clear distinction between the secular and commercial space of the streets and the sacred and devotional space of the cathedral. We feel, or at least those of us do who are not devout pilgrims, an abrupt transition as we enter the cathedral: we have entered a sanctuary of belief and left behind the surrounding places of business. Or, to describe this transition in different terms, our experience of entering the building registers a strict distinction: the sacred has retreated to the cathedral precincts and commerce has taken over the streets. As Fassler observes in her detailed study, however, the *Adventus* procession moved through the streets of medieval Chartres and in so doing reminded all present that these same streets were also sacred space. By reenacting Christian history, this ritual procession through the streets of Chartres makes sacred events from the past—events, one must remember, scripted within the terms of holy writ—visible and present to that community. In this way, a procession endows these same events with a high degree of reverence because the ceremony is so carefully staged, and also with a striking measure of drama because the ceremony is so vividly present.

The workings of this ceremony transformed the space of daily life so that the cathedral of a French town could become a type of the Temple of Jerusalem. In reconstructing the *Adventus* procession from afar, we must follow Fassler in recognizing the importance of its various ceremonial elements: the sanctifying presence of holy relics, the glamour of ecclesiastical robes, the songs of those processing through the streets. For those of the Christian faith, the procession engaged their attention and reverence through an active appeal to their senses. Distances of historical time are elided, figural associations of belief are reinforced, and the presence of the faith is registered devoutly. And, as a salutary reminder of cultural difference, we must also register the presence of those who would have found the ceremony theologically disturbing, if not, in fact, physically threatening. The Jewish population of Chartres would have had a very different reading of the *Adventus* procession than did those who performed it or witnessed it from within the Christian community. To the Jews of Chartres, the procession would have carried the stigma of exclusion, and more, of demonization. The example of Chartres, as Fassler presents it, reminds us that a medieval community was often in fact several intertwined communities and thus a ceremonial enactment could well evoke radically contradictory responses from those who witnessed it with awe or with aversion. Contemporary scholars of pre-modern Europe must, as this cautionary example suggests, resist the practice of depicting the past as a culture possessed of both a ritualistic homogeneity and social harmony that elude us in our own world. Ceremonies exclude just as much as they include, and those excluded are as deserving of scholarly attention as those included. Only sentimentalists can lament the loss of such ceremonies because only they can forget their power to divide as well as to unite.

That the same ceremony could be read by observers in very different—even antagonistic—ways emerges as well from Michael Flier's searching examination of the Epiphany and Palm Sunday rituals in medieval Moscow, "Seeing Is Believing: The Semiotics of Dynasty and Destiny in Muscovite Rus'." Flier begins by tracing the literal path of these processions through the city as they began at the Cathedral of the Dormition and then moved "south from this locus through the gates of the Tainitsky Tower of the Kremlin wall out onto the frozen ice of the Moscow River, symbolizing the River Jordan." The power of ceremonial processions to inscribe sacred history onto the local terrain of belief is captured beautifully at the performative level of these processions. Perhaps the most telling sign of the ceremony's local nature is its enactment on a frozen river: it cannot be performed anytime or anywhere. Also noteworthy is the adaptation of local flora for this ritual by which the exotic and virtually unobtainable palm of the Holy Land was often replaced by the familiar and abundant willow of Muscovite Rus'. The flora differ but both signify early blooming trees and thus harbingers of spring and so, more spiritually, of the Resurrection. In this case at least, the signs may differ in outward physical form and place of origin but function in the same way as signifiers. Indeed, the translation from palm to willow does not so much disrupt the ceremony as render it locally efficacious in a specific time and place. That the details of a ceremony can assist the imagination of those who observe it emerges beautifully from Flier's description. So, too, the replacement of the ass ridden by Christ with a horse disguised as an ass led by the secular ruler reflects local conditions being transformed in light of the historical narrative of Christ's public ministry. The power of ceremony to elevate the local—the frozen Moscow River—into the universal—the baptismal waters of the Jordan—establishes the landscape of belief in visible and thus believable ways. As Flier argues throughout, seeing was believing in the culture of medieval Rus' and nothing made seeing more compelling, and thus belief more possible, than reenactments of events from sacred history set in public space.

That these reenactments in Muscovite Rus' drew their terms from the established iconography of Christ's life, especially as it represented events in Jerusalem, gave them great power to shape the belief of those who witnessed the Epiphany and Palm Sunday rituals. Through public ceremonies, the secular and sacred powers of the culture—the tsar and the metropolitan—created rituals that taught Christian history but also promised "a remarkable destiny for this latter-day Chosen People," that is, a glorious Apocalypse in Rus'. Ceremony can be seen in this instance as defining the territorial realm of those who participate in it because it has symbolic value across all of Rus', not simply where it was performed in Moscow. Within the intended terms and meanings of the Epiphany and Palm Sunday rituals, these two forms of power were brought into a balanced relation: both tsar and metropolitan had his place in the glorious future envisioned for their people. As events developed, however, this unified interpretation of the Apocalypse became a ground for controversy between the ruling elite and the dissident Old Believers. Ceremonies meant to instill religious orthodoxy and political unity took on a different function when competing images of the "tsar's role in the End Times" became fiercely contested. Yet whether the tsar was Savior or Antichrist, it was through ceremony that each side "competed visually and verbally for the hearts and minds of the Muscovite faithful throughout the seventeenth century." Yet again, one must point to the power of ceremonies to divide rather than unify, to cause dissension rather than harmony.

No one over a certain age can read Flier's study of ceremonial processions through Moscow without remembering images from the recent past—at least from before 1989—of May Day parades with marching soldiers, missile launchers, and rumbling tanks passing beneath the walls of this same Kremlin. The nature of these ceremonies has changed radically; the beliefs that each enact differ in readily apparent ways. And yet the ritual space for each is the same. Through such memories of place we can sometimes connect in unexpected ways with the once-potent rituals of the past. Or we can better understand that a specific location in a given society can become so charged with a ceremonial aura that it must be used by those who openly seek to assert their power, whether it be spiritual, military, political, or, in some combination of these, nationalist. A capital may be defined, at least in some way, as the necessary place for enacting ceremonies, regardless of the form they embody or the beliefs they promulgate.

The increasing politicization of ceremony that Flier begins to trace in regard to Muscovite Rus' emerges as an explicit subject in Gordon Kipling's "The King's Advent Transformed: The Consecration of the City in the

Sixteenth-Century Civic Triumph." Kipling begins by establishing that the staged entry of the future Emperor Charles V into Bruges in 1515 was designed to be seen as a "type of Christ's entry into Jerusalem." The spaces of the city, its streets and squares, become the setting for a political allegory or, depending on the emphasis one places on the terms of the procession, for an allegorized politics. Either way, the entry of 1515 becomes, in Kipling's reading, the type for later processions of that same form, especially that of Prince Philip into Antwerp in 1549. This process of modeling one enactment of a ritualized ceremony on an earlier version speaks to the ceremony's power to create precedent, even if the precedent needs to be modified over time to accommodate more immediate and local circumstances. So too, this process of modeling reminds one that all ceremonies are, when seen from a sufficient distance, invented at a certain moment rather than inevitable in the order of things. The highly theatrical staging of a political entry could be made to assert publicly the force of precedent, because it was there to be witnessed by any and all who belonged to the place. Thus, as Kipling shows, the obeisance of Antwerp to Philip was established through the figure of the "Antwerp Giant, Druon Antigon," that had come to embody the tyrannical abuse of power. The 1549 procession featured a giant "in the form of a colossal statue which, by mechanical means, rolls its eyeballs, then nods its head as a sign of reverence for Philip." The dramatic allegory conveyed by the staging is apparent: the tyrannical past, embodied in the monstrous form of a giant, reverently gives way to the benign and enlightened rule of Philip. The element of national difference here should also be stressed: Philip was of Spain, and Antwerp was as a city subject to that foreign power.

When in 1582, a generation or so later, the cities of the Netherlands revolted against their Spanish overlords, they asserted their political identity by choosing their own compatriots to rule them. Thus Antwerp selected Francis of Anjou to become its lord, and welcomed him into the city with a *joyeuse entrée*. Among the elaborate pageantry and ritual that greeted him was a reappearance of that same "Antwerp Giant, Druon Antigon." Greeting Francis in the marketplace of Antwerp, the signifying giant not only nodded his head in reverence but lowered with one hand the arms of Spain and with the other raised the arms of Anjou. This advance in the giant's mechanical ability was meant to signal the advancement of political justice and liberty under the new regime, but that message of political progress gained its propagandistic force because it was encoded in traditional imagery. The enduring presence of the giant in this ceremonial entry serves to legitimate the act of Netherlandish rebellion against the tyrannies of Spain. Through repetition, ceremony establishes its enduring power; through telling variations within that same repetition, ceremony remains vital and responsive to political change. Or, while the presence of the Antwerp Giant may be a common feature of these two political entries, the meaning it acquires or displays to those observing it shifts considerably. No doubt the same supporter of Spanish rule who in 1549 took pleasure at witnessing its political allegiance and mechanical cleverness would have been horrified by its change of sympathies in 1582. But such a change of response is in its own way another reminder that ceremony should not be seen simply as the mere repetition of empty gestures and coded meanings, as bound to display only the dead hand of the past. Ceremony may not have a life of its own, but those who manage it can rearrange its forms, allegiances, and even meanings for their own purposes and can do so without necessarily diminishing its power. Sometimes, indeed, they make it more powerful by updating its signification while preserving its outward or visible forms.

If Kipling's study alerts us to the fact that ceremonies are not fixed in meaning over time, it also suggests that political ceremonies are by their nature subject to varying interpretations—even though they are intended to be unifying in their effects. Focusing on Italy in his "The Eye of the Procession: Ritual Ways of Seeing in the Renaissance," Edward Muir turns his attention to the ways in which procession and other forms of ritual are dichotomous and ambiguous, and thus how they respond to variant interpretations. Or, as he says in a provocative claim, "I wish to suggest that the struggle to affix a consistent meaning to ritual was a vain quest because it is the very defiance of uniform meaning while evoking powerful emotions that produces the lure of ritual." By drawing on Renaissance optical theory, Muir argues for a highly dynamic nature of processions and other ceremonies. Viewers of such events were, in effect, irradiated with "beneficent spiritual or authoritarian influences" that emanated from the procession they were watching. Processions were public phenomena precisely because they radiated such influences; they were not simply to be witnessed passively but were to be experienced actively. Moreover, viewers of processions were not only gazing outward at those participating in the processions; they were also being gazed at by those in the processions. Facile distinctions between the seeing subject and the seen object cannot hold when one considers the dynamics of processions through the streets of Renaissance Italian cities. The incipient volatility of such processions, their "dangerous social potential to metamorphose from ritual order to ritual riot," makes them speak not simply to the means by which established authority asserted its interpretation of spiritual and political questions, but also to the community's sometimes dissenting or rebellious responses to these same interpretations.

Muir's conclusion, that a certain instability of meaning is necessary if rituals are to maintain their excitement and energy, offers a powerful interpretive insight. It explains how some events do not become, in his telling phrase, the "big yawn" of empty ritual but instead retain their vitality. Those who participate in the same ritual over and over again within the course of their lifetimes are not, by Muir's reading, automatons following the same script in mindless ways. Indeed, the example of the Antwerp Giant suggests that even a mechanical contrivance can change its role in a political ceremony! Processions, rituals, and the like are profound symbolic acts because they allow their participants to negotiate and renegotiate questions of meaning inherent in matters of spiritual or political urgency. Such negotiations and renegotiations necessarily involved both those who processed as public figures (whether in sacred or secular roles) and those who, by witnessing such processions, constituted its community. The meaning of the ceremony resided not simply in the performance, but also in those who made up its audience. Part of that meaning, though not necessarily in an official manner, concerns the power of ceremonies to contain a hint of the anarchic and the lawless that give them an edge of excitement, even of danger.

As even my brief summaries of the chapters in this volume demonstrate, processions, dramas, rituals, and liturgies confound our easy distinctions between the public and the private, for these forms are alike in being able to transform the places of daily life, such as streets, city squares, and even frozen rivers, into spaces filled with sacral and charismatic power. Religious and political processions are especially effective means for displaying the mysteries of belief and the aura of power. In ways that no written text can quite manifest, even in cultures that are deeply shaped by literacy, ceremony strives to create agreement and consent just as it also opens itself to the possibility of dissonance and dissent. But ceremonies are not opposed to texts. They often depend quite literally on texts for their statements and iconographies, but they move out of the sphere of readerly activity to the shared sites of a community or group.

One cannot help speculating that ceremonies may often have offered some relief from the inwardness of textual culture, that is, they must have seemed especially welcome as public manifestations of ideas and beliefs that were not restricted to those possessing the skills of literacy. Moreover, ceremonies are performances and thus have their own forms of choreography about them that yield a certain kinesthetic pleasure to those who participate in them. Anyone who has ever observed children as they watch and imitate figures in a parade knows that such kinesthetic pleasures can also be shared by those observing the ceremony.

Processions, as they demonstrate the mobility and thus the potential ubiquity of sacred and political power, affect the sense that most people have of their environs. Spaces that for most days of the year are sites of commerce and communal life can become the setting for ceremonies that speak to the most pressing questions of this life and the next. Processions, as they move displays of power out of palace and church, the sites typically reserved for them, remind us that conventional distinctions between public and private may sometimes be no more than the necessary fictions of a secular, democratic society. Put another way, the case studies presented in this volume remind us that the distinctions we often struggle to maintain between the sacred and secular, the private and the public, the daily and the performative are drawn very rigidly for reasons having largely to do with our contemporary concerns. These pairings need not be binary oppositions; their terms need not be defined through an antagonism that forces one term to obscure or obliterate the other. The ceremony of a street procession led by archbishop or prince serves instead to remind us that the categories of the sacred and secular, the private and the public, the daily and the performative are permeable and fluid in their use of space as well as in their duration in time. Or, from another perspective, ceremonies and rituals mattered in the past and continue to matter in the present because they are not reducible to simple interpretation. That they earn their claims on their original participants and audiences through complexity and fluidity is a necessary counter to the common assumption that holds ceremony must always be hegemonic, elitist, oppressive. Not all ceremonies are "mere rituals," to use the derogatory cliché that has rhetorical force only because some rituals are the necessary ceremonies of life.

There is much to be said then for what one might call the expert knowledge of ceremonies: that is, the understanding of the viewer who has witnessed multiple instances of the same ceremony and thus who has grown alive to its variations and continuities. At times, that expertise must have included the recognition that ceremonies, as they assert a necessary claim, also contain the possibility of its undoing. Thus, the triumphal entry of a new ruler not only declares his power but also seeks to repress the possibility that not everyone within the community will accept that power. The social energy of a procession or other ritual cannot always be contained easily once it has been dispersed into a larger group that is not strictly of one mind. The performance of a ceremony may well contain the possibility of acting out or of social disruption as in the demonstrations of the contemporary AIDS activist organization ACT UP (AIDS Coalition to Unleash Power). That is the remarkable double life of ceremonial culture: it displays in full view of a community the manifestation of an otherwise ineffable idea or belief, and thus the potential to reject or otherwise modify both idea and manifestation. And through this process, of course, another ceremony is created.

NOTES

1. Michel de Certeau, *The Practice of Everyday Life,* trans. Steven Rendall (Berkeley: University of California Press, 1988), 31.

2. The chapters in this book were originally presented as lectures in a series sponsored by the Center for Medieval and Renaissance Studies at the Ohio State University when I served as its director.

Adventus at Chartres

Ritual Models for Major Processions

MARGOT FASSLER

Adventus: An Introduction

Adventus is the fundamental ritual structure underlying the great majority of liturgical processions and public ceremonies of the antique
and the medieval Christian worlds. "Arrival," the "entrance" of great
and important figures, stimulates human interest: every feature of an
adventus is calculated to provoke awe and stir curiosity. Those present
witness not only grand and prominent people on parade. In major festivals, the crowd was (and is) almost as important as those feted, as every
observer gets to explore ranges of reaction found in people of all layers of
society, lined up—in some sort of order or not—on either side of the
red carpet or its rush-strewn equivalent. The legacy is long. Bridal processions, triumphant receptions of sports or military heroes, the opening
convocations at schools, the firemen's field day parades (that sometimes
feature beer tents as their final destinations)—all these familiar ritual
structures, or at least elements of them, are directly dependent upon formulae borrowed from the ancient *adventus*.[1]

    A classic *adventus* has three major components: (1) a gathering and
arranging of those who will receive the person or persons coming;

(2) the coming in itself, which commonly features some sort of procession; and (3) a ceremony of reception by prominent persons, who will then escort the one received to a destination for vows or other formal actions and sometimes for the exchange of tokens or other regalia. The structure of the medieval ceremony has been studied by Noël Coulet in a provocative article that observes shifting attitudes toward Jewish participation as reflected in the *adventus* from various places and times.[2] She also notes the longevity of the ceremony and criticizes works that downplay or ignore the power of early traditions in the later Middle Ages.[3] Not only do changes in details of ceremonies reveal societal transformations of various sorts, the ceremony itself allowed for the re-creation of events from the past and the hailing of people who lived long ago. Relics were very often received with an *adventus,* and this allowed saints to be experienced as actually present in the midst of adoring crowds.[4] So, too, with re-creations of episodes in the lives of Christ and of other figures; Christ, symbolically re-created through the power of *adventus,* walked the earth once again every year in the major processions of the church year. In his essay on the nature of processional liturgies in twelfth-century Rome, Sible de Blaauw distinguishes the cortege, the procession made by the pope or his substitute during the stational liturgy, from participatory processions, and studies both in regard to occasions, actors, modes of progression, vestments and attributes, order of participants, topography, and ceremonial.[5] His work is an excellent introduction to the subject and its various elements without pointing to *adventus* as the underlying ritual structure of his topic.

As might be expected, the complex and far-reaching subject of *adventus* has attracted much attention from scholars of both antique and medieval cultures. The kinds of processions and greetings associated with *adventus* ceremonies in particular have called to students of ritual as well as to historians.[6] The formal ways in which leaders of societies were hailed and received express fundamental human relationships, both in the past and in the present.[7] These events, with their texts and music, offered opportunities for communities from every age to reconstruct dramatic events from the past as they recast them in their own times. The identification of art works that depict *adventus* ceremonies, or that were themselves used in these rituals, has proven, too, that this is an interdisciplinary subject by its very nature.

An introduction to the topic is provided here through reference to a group of select *adventus* ceremonies, some of which are famous, some not, but few of which have been studied as embodiments of the genre. The first two make the point that the ceremonies, with their common elements, were referenced and celebrated throughout the late antique and medieval periods. A description of a royal *adventus* or "arrival" dated to 585 found in the writings of Gregory of Tours depicts the coming of the Frankish king Guntram into Orleans.[8] If this well-known passage is contrasted with Chrétien de Troyes' description of King Arthur found in *Yvain,* many of the same elements are present.[9] However far removed the two passages are from each other in time and genre, clearly they depict the same thing: a ceremonial action of triumphant entrance and greeting. The acclamations, music, festive banners, and singing along the route accompany the subject; a leader comes forth to greet him; subsequently he is escorted to a formal ceremony.

By the eleventh century customaries, ordinals, and pontificals contain outlines of *adventus* rites for kings or queens, bishops, abbots, and other secular and ecclesiastical leaders. As a fairly detailed description of an ideal *adventus* ceremony found in the mid-eleventh-century Cluniac customary prepared for the imperial Abbey of Farfa shows, the ceremony defines relationships, and those welcomed give as well as receive.[10] The procession going out to meet the king and escort him into the church was surely flanked by people who hailed the royal party; here, too, the singing plays a prominent role. With liturgical documents prepared by cantors themselves, we can often tell by what was actually sung and read the significance of the text and sometimes of the type of music or style of singing. In the ceremony at Farfa, the cantor was given some leeway in the choice of chants, but some were clearly specified:

> *For leading in the King:* When the *adventus regis* into the monastery has been announced, with either the abbot or the prior telling the brothers, if there is not time for speaking in the cloister let all be gathered in the church. And all will put on copes, even the *conversi,* and the children will be clothed in tunics. Let the secretaries make ready the procession. And then the two largest bells will be rung. The opening of the processional line is to be ordered as follows:

Cross	Holy Water	Cross
Thurible	Cross	Thurible
Candelabrum	Book	Candelabrum
Candelabrum	Book	Candelabrum
Candelabrum	Book	Candelabrum

Next the *conversi* process two by two, then the children with their teachers, then the lord abbot and then all the brethren, two by two just as above, except that they are silent. When they come to the King, let the abbot give him holy water and let him kiss the book and be incensed. Then let the responsory "Ecce mitto angelum meum" ("Behold I send my angel") be intoned and the servants ring all the bells. In the church two carpets are arranged, one before the altar of the Holy Cross and the other before the main altar. Then the abbot intones the antiphon or responsory that he finds appropriate. When that has been sung, let him read the chapter of Scripture and these prayers: "Omnipotens sempiterne deus qui caelestia simul et terrena moderaris" and another "Omnipotens sempiterne deus miserere famulo tuo." And let them process back into the cloister. For the Queen, let them do the same thing, except that when going into the church they sing the antiphon "Cum sederit filius hominis."

The prescriptive description of a formal reception provides the leader with a time to be blessed and to pay homage to the relics of the church and to the altar of the Cross. Particularly notable is the chant sung when the king is entering the church. The text of the responsory "Ecce mitto angelum meum" (borrowed from the Lenten office) is taken from the tables of laws and promises offered by God to Moses (Exodus 23:20: "Behold I will send my angel, which shall go before thee, and keep thee in thy journey, and bring thee into the place that I have prepared)."[11] Understood in its scriptural context the chant promises a secular ruler protection from God if the ruler behaves justly and obeys the laws established for him to follow. Both welcome and warning are here, and indeed when churches and monasteries were displeased with their rulers, the processional reception was often denied. The ruler was at once both supreme and obedient; he fell down before altars and kissed relics, and yet was hailed with a ceremonial dignity that sometimes represented a major expenditure for the community doing the receiving. If the queen was received a different chant was sung, the antiphon "Cum sederit filius hominis,"[12] the opening of which comes from Matthew 19:28 (those who follow Christ will "sit on the seat of his majesty"). The queen, too, is heralded as one whose office has been earned by faithfulness.

The *adventus* ceremony of the ancient world, upon which a host of welcoming ceremonies in medieval Christian Europe were based, provided an opportunity not only to welcome triumphant leaders and their entourages but also established the framework for the exchange of presents and greetings between various political and religious contingents. *Adventus* functioned in both sacred and secular realms, and processions in this mode are infused with ideals of kingship, priesthood, and sainthood.[13] Even in antique cultures *adventus* processions often included gestures of obedience, symbolic actions capable of making peace.[14]

But the sense of power was often heightened by the display of losers as well as winners, and occasionally featured the torture and death of conquered peoples, making the ceremony a play with real consequences.[15] The Maya of Bonampak, for example, painted a vivid mural of a triumphant procession c. 800.[16] General details of the procession, which included what must have been cacophonous musical performances, featured public torture and the ceremonial killing of captives as well as a magnificent hailing of the victorious leader.[17] *Adventus* ceremonies such as this, whether in Greece, Rome, or the ancient New World, gave crowds an opportunity to examine the spoils of the wars they had suffered through, lost loved ones in, or been taxed for, and to jeer human captives whose suffering was experienced as retribution (at least by some members of the crowd). A famous *adventus* from the first century provides a dramatic example of the varying emotions in the same ritual action: Christ was hailed at the beginning of one week as a triumphant leader; by the close of the week he was paraded to an ignominious death.[18] Shakespeare's *Coriolanus* explores the *adventus* and varying public opinion reflected in the tone and structure of the ceremony as rulers fell in and out of favor.[19]

The deeply ingrained *adventus* ceremony allowed for endless ways of manipulating its details to make meaning, from the healing of strife to the acceptance of new relationships.[20] The ceremony could be altered to make a statement about the ruler or the people; flaws could indicate the failure of relationships. The eleventh-century Burgundian historian Rodulfus Glaber describes the reception of the German emperor Henry II in Rome for the purpose of receiving the regalia of his office, which included the golden orb, bestudded with jewels. After a magnificent procession the splendid items were offered; the emperor turned the orb in his hands, and then proclaimed that those worthy of it are those "who trample underfoot the pomps of this world," and offered this symbol of his power to the monks of Cluny.[21]

In his life of King Louis VI, Abbot Suger mentions several *adventus* ceremonies, one of which demonstrates how variations in tone or other elements of the ceremony could portend disaster. He describes the reception of the emperor Henry V in Rome by Pope Pascal, with significant detail:

> Wearing fine capes, they rode horses draped with white cloths and has-
> tened to meet the emperor, and the Roman people were trailing behind.
> The pope had already sent ahead envoys who received the emperor's
> oath, taken on the most holy Gospels, that he would preserve the peace
> and put aside the quarrel over investitures. . . . And the Romans enjoyed
> a wonderful scene when the emperor himself and his magnates extended
> their hands and swore it a third time on the very porch of the church.
> There next took place a ceremony more splendid by far than if some-
> one were being graced by a triumphal arch after winning a victory in
> Africa. The most holy hands of the lord pope placed the imperial di-
> adem on the emperor's head in the style of the Augusti amid triumphal
> hymns of praise. And with a large crowd devoutly looking on, the em-
> peror was led with great solemnity to the most holy altar of the apostles
> while the clergy sang hymns before him and the Germans shouted out
> frightening chants that pierced the heavens. . . .[22]

The "frightening chants" are foreboding: soon after the ceremony, the Germans attacked the pope and his entourage, extorting annulments of pledges made earlier. The Germans were playing a false role in the *adventus,* intending to violate its agreements with actions whose harshness was signaled by the style of the singing.[23]

With a ritual action so well integrated into the fabric of public life, opportunities for play and reversal abounded. Everyone would understand when the most solemn *adventus* receptions and processions—those at which the *laudes regiae* were intoned for the king,[24] or at the heralding and procession of bishops in medieval cathedral towns—were turned inside out. In the early thirteenth-century *Play of Daniel* from the cathedral of Beauvais Babylonian kings were escorted with lavish and loud processions as the greeting "Rex in eternum vive" resounded to hail their *adventus* and their actions. But each is killed in turn, rendering the processions and greeting ironic.[25] The song "Orientis partibus," with its barked out "hez, hez," was featured in many mock *adventus* ceremonies in the seasons of Advent and Christmas, hailing the ass and escorting a boy bishop to perform traditional actions with various twists.[26] In the Daniel play, elements from *adventus* ceremonies for kings and for bishops are mingled, as one of the kings is fooled and quotes music from "Orientis partibus" as he himself becomes the ass of the season.[27]

Major Processions of the Church Year: The Example of Chartres

Medieval Chartres, like many northern cathedral towns, sustained a rich processional life, as Table 1 in the appendix demonstrates. The cathedral was a great heart that pumped clergy and people forth into the town and drew them back into itself after the appropriate stations were made.[28] As the ordinals and other liturgical books demonstrate, external processions almost always departed with chants that referred to the destination, the place where a station would be made (and often part of the day's liturgy celebrated), while the return and approach to the cathedral were always accompanied by the singing of Marian chants.[29] A life-long resident of the town would have known where a procession was going just by the sounds issuing from the singers' mouths. Also, because there was a consistent rhythm to the processions, even subtle variations in their modes could be perceived as symbolic. Amid the constant comings and goings of this stational liturgy, relationships between the various ecclesial communities were defined, as was the role of the bishop himself, the leader of the diocese.[30]

Adventus and the ceremonies connected with it were transformed in the twelfth century in northern Europe by the great numbers of new sculpted portals added to older churches, and constructed as significant features of new churches as well. The grandiose programs that were carried out in this century made every new door a triumphal arch, the "crowds" of figures providing an *adventus* throng for every procession, major and minor.[31] The bishop or abbot and his entourage, the king or queen, the count or countess, all were welcomed into the nave of the church with a new pomp that only paralleled the desired numbers of congregants who were now joined by replicas of kings, queens, bishops, and prophets. Sculpted *jubés* or rood screens became the backdrop for internal processions and, like their counterparts outside, welcomed the entourage that moved into the choir. At Chartres, where so much of the sculpted portal survives and the liturgy of the twelfth century is documented by a contemporary ordinal, we have a unique opportunity to study the medieval *adventus* ceremony, not only through liturgical texts and ritual actions, but also through the ways in which the ceremony was made to be interactive with the Royal Portal. With such artistic and liturgical sources, Chartres is an attractive subject for scholars, but the processions studied in this essay were universal in the Latin Middle Ages.[32] Their model is the *adventus* ceremony, and the liturgy of Advent itself, a subject I have analyzed as yet another complex framework for the reception of a powerful king.[33] The Chartrain processions, and others as well, have not hitherto been compared and studied under the rubric of *adventus,* yet it is fundamental to each of them, and each bends tradition to make meanings for the participants. Although the festive rhythms of *adventus* can be seen to operate on many levels and to be associated with numerous liturgical practices, from the organization of the season of Advent itself to the openings of major parts of the Mass liturgy, especially in the rites for entering the church,[34] at the Gospel procession that marked the "entrance" of the Word,[35] and the offertory hailing the presence of Christ at Eucharist, *adventus* is especially apparent in the three feasts to be studied here: Purification, Palm Sunday, and Ascension.

All Christians in the central Middle Ages—lay, clerical, or monastic— experienced *adventus* on a regular basis through these feasts, and their structures in Chartres in the mid-twelfth century can serve as representative of similar situations in northern Europe more generally. Every Christian person in the community had a part to play in these three feasts, at least as "extras" in the crowd scenes. But unlike *adventus* ceremonies for living kings and queens—like that from Farfa noted above—the ruler was not physically present in these rites. This in itself made these liturgical *adventus* ceremonies strikingly different from their secular counterparts, allowing the dramatic framework to shift with festive conditions, and the roles of royal personages and the members of their entourages to be taken on by many individuals. The emblems of the feast in each case aid in the ritual re-presentation of a ruler present only in spirit, and the processions suggest ways in which liturgical symbolism functioned in medieval art and ceremony. Moreover, because all three ceremonies were based on stories in the Bible and biblical exegesis, they offered Christians in every town numerous opportunities to reenact historical events, and thereby to remember them, both as individuals and as communities.[36] This constant replication of the past was fundamental to how the Bible was known in the Middle Ages and to how history was "made" and comprehended by medieval people.[37] The three feasts discussed here are all about coming in and going out, about moving across and through symbolic doors and gateways, and into and out of glorious spaces—the Temple and its imagined counterpart in heavenly Jerusalem—and about the boundaries between the realms of time and space, of life and of death. Rites of passage are also fundamental to how *adventus* works, with a ruler entering a town through its major portal or a church through its major door, just as the Messiah was seen to "enter" the world of time and human existence, transform it, and then leave to regain a heavenly throne. The entire season of Advent, itself a massive *adventus,* with the characters featured in its texts and chants gathering to witness the birth of the king, provides yet another framework for the ceremonies studied here.[38]

We should not be surprised that the three feasts celebrating *adventus* most dramatically in medieval Chartres—the Purification, Palm Sunday, and the Ascension—also were the loci of the three major festive processions of the church year, with certain features distinguishing them one from another. When processions took the entire worshipping community outside the confines of sacred space, by necessity they were carefully planned. From the texts and rubrics for processions supplied in various liturgical books we can gain an understanding of how people moved, what they sang and heard sung, and what they saw during a clerical or monastic community's most intensely public hours.[39] The dramatic processions of the church year, always reenactments of historic events, shaped both popular and clerical imaginations, placing scripture and saints' lives on parade.[40] Attendance of all Christians was expected at every major feast: a miracle story from the twelfth century in circulation at Chartres describes the withering of the hand of a woman who decided to stay home and weave on a feast day instead of going to church;[41] cathedrals were built large enough to accommodate the local populace and pilgrims on days of major festivals, and fairs often coincided with major feasts.[42] Processions, frequently interactive with artworks and altars, also made statements about the prosperity and well-being of the town. They included the display of ancient books, gold and silver reliquaries, elaborate crosses, and jewels of great value. These furnishings reinforced the idea that the messages and events embodied in the action were both deeply important and also were particular to the community and its history.

Richard of St. Victor, in the third quarter of the twelfth century, wrote a commentary on the three major processions of the church year. His treatise relates their action to the exercise of worship by the entire community, helping to identify the distinct character of each of the feasts as they were understood in the Middle Ages itself. Although Richard's commentary is an allegorical exercise, it nonetheless directs attention to various features of the ceremonial, and incorporates processional action into the larger sense of each soul's pilgrimage toward greater closeness with God:

> These three feasts, we know well, have these things in common: among the numerous processions of the year or of each week which we celebrate solemnly, these are the primary processions, and the best attended. The first feast concerns what happens at the time of purification when a baby was brought by its parents to the Temple. The second takes its origin from the day wherein Jesus climbed with his disciples from Bethany to the fortress-like city which lay before them. The third takes its institution from the moment when Jesus, having led his disciples onto the Mount of Olives, was raised before their eyes into heaven.[43]

Richard goes on to describe the attributes of each feast, the festive props that the people held in their hands during the processions: for the Purification, lighted candles; for Palm Sunday, green branches and flowers; and for the Ascension, banners and crosses. Each of these has allegorical significance, but also relates to the historical sense of any event reenacted in a stylized way. Although the elements making up the three feasts were in place by the ninth century, each community came to celebrate feasts such as these with slight variations in detail, emphasizing some features and not others. Celebrating in any community not one's own would have held special interest to those attuned to nuances of ceremony, chant, and the visual arts: all would have been essentially the same, but the surface of the ritual would have been ever in flux, and astute pilgrims would have been able to sense regional variations in the liturgical menus through close study of the evidence. For larger towns, with great preachers and teachers, the sense would have been defined with even more piquant local flavor, as was surely the case in the years of the greatest Chartrain bishops, Fulbert in the early eleventh century and Ivo and Geoffrey in the twelfth century. Their preaching defined tradition, while it also offered views of what *adventus* in the liturgy meant during this period. Descriptions of the ceremonial in the three feasts described below have two components: sung liturgical texts that were in place by the late ninth century, and interpretations of these texts through the public ceremonies and preaching that we know took place in Chartres and that developed in the eleventh and early twelfth centuries. Each is fundamentally an *adventus;* in its turn, the sculpture program of the Royal Portal depends to a degree on each of these feasts and was designed to receive their festive processions.

The Procession for the Purification: Entering the Temple

The biblical account of *Hypapante* (the Meeting) — or the Purification of the Blessed Virgin Mary, as it came to be known in the West — is found in Luke's Gospel alone. The story itself constitutes an early Christian view of ancient practices, drawing upon materials from the Old Testament and deliberately creating strong parallels between Hannah and Samuel and Mary and Jesus.[44] Luke conflates two practices, the offering of a first-born son to the Temple and the rite of purification a woman had to undergo after giving birth in order to be able to attend services once again. Raymond Brown says that the historically problematic scene in Luke results from a combination of inaccurate knowledge of the exact customs, and from a conflict between the two motifs: "Luke was writing about practices he knew only from Scripture, and not with first-hand knowledge."[45] Medieval liturgical reenactments of biblical stories, such as this one from Luke, were frequently able to move beyond the problems of a literal comparison between details in the Old Testament and the New (or between the Synoptic Gospels) to proclaim the dramatic essences of events, as is the case with the procession on February 2. Ironically, liturgical reenactments were then sometimes used in later medieval exegesis to explain problems within the texts themselves; liturgical reenactment offered everyone a steady interpretation of various features of the texts. In this case, the action as defined by the chant texts was not concerned primarily with the purification rite itself, but rather with the idea that Mary carried her son in her hands, that Symeon received him, and that Anna the prophetess acknowledged his presence.

As Egeria, the fourth-century nun and traveler, described it, the feast was originally of the Lord and was designed to fall forty days after the celebration of Christ's birth, which in late fourth-century Jerusalem took place on January 6 (the multi-thematic feast of the Epiphany).[46] From the middle of the fifth century the Jerusalem celebration was marked by a procession in which people carried lighted candles, a feature of the festal celebration that later shaped its character throughout the West as well. As liturgical texts and commentaries on them, as well as sermon literature, demonstrate, each person who processes and carries a candle typifies the Virgin Mary, and the light carried represents the Messiah, brought by human hands into his dwelling place, the Temple. The welcoming greeters in this *adventus* ceremony, Symeon and Anna, are old and righteous, and they have waited for this King all of their lives. At Chartres and throughout Europe the candles themselves were blessed and distributed to the clergy and people to the chanting of Symeon's epithets for Christ: *Lumen ad revelationem gentium* and *gloriam plebis tuae Israel,* "the light for the revelation of the gentiles" and "the glory of your people Israel." The connection with Symeon was not emphasized only through chant texts: at St. Denis the abbot blessed the candles with the relic of St. Symeon's arm, which was carried by the deacon in the procession.[47] The bishop's prayers over the candles at Chartres described their significance as well and related them to both Mary, the Christbearer, and to Symeon, the receiver.[48]

The three antiphons sung during the procession at Chartres (and elsewhere throughout Europe) determined the nature of the action and revealed the powerful feelings of the major characters, making it possible and likely that medieval participants attempted to re-create wonder within themselves through association. The first two processional antiphons listed in the sources were imported from the East and appear in some early western liturgical books in both Latin and Greek.[49] Thus the ancient ceremony is explained by chant texts known in the Middle Ages to be very old and to have come, like the feast itself, from other regions.[50] Chants and texts such as these were sung relics of the past, venerable *spolia* of other cultures, embraced and adapted throughout the Christian West, and renewed through their festive performances every year. These texts were sung as the clergy and people processed in circular motion at Chartres, most likely inside the nave of the cathedral, but then, certainly, through a door to the outside.[51] In the first antiphon Mary is hailed as the Theotokos; in the second, her bridal bed is the new Jerusalem of the church; Symeon is present in both texts, as the receiver of the anointed king:

Ave gracia plena dei genitrix virgo, ex te enim ortus est sol iusticie, illuminansque in tenebris sunt; letare tu senior iuste suscipens ihesum in ulnas liberatorem animarum nostrarum donantem nobis et resurrectionem.

——

[Hail, full of grace, virgin genetrix of God: from you has risen the Sun of justice, illuminating those who are in darkness; rejoice you just old man, as you take Jesus, the liberator of our souls, in your arms, as he bestows the resurrection on us.]

Adorna thalamum tuum syon et suscipe regem cristum; amplectere mariam que est celestis porta ipsa enim portat regem glorie nouo lumine subsisti virgo adducens in manibus filium ante luciferum [genitum] quem accipiens symeon in ulnas suas predicauit populus dominum deum esse uite et mortis et sauatorem [salvatorem] mundi.

——

[Adorn your bridal bed, Sion, and receive the anointed one, the King; embrace Mary, who is the gate of heaven, for she carries the King of glory with new light; remaining ever a virgin, she brings in her hands the Son begotten before the daystar; whom Symeon, taking him into his arms, proclaimed to the people to be the Lord God of life and death, and the Saviour of the world.]

Once outside, the clergy and people lined up in front of the west portal, which was called the "Royal Portal" even in twelfth-century Chartres.
At this point a third antiphon was sung, while the clergy and people faced
the door:[52]

> Responsum accepit symeon a spiritu sancto non uisurum se mortem
> nisi uideret cristum domini et cum inducerent puerum in templo ac-
> cepit eum in ulnas suas et bendxcit [benedixit] deum et dixit nunc
> dimittis domine seruum tuum in pace.

> ———

> [Simeon received an answer from the Holy Spirit that he would not
> see death before he had seen the Anointed of the Lord; and when they
> brought the child into the Temple, he took him into his arms and blessed
> God and said: Now, Lord, dismiss your servant in peace.]

This *adventus* ceremony first prepares a bridal bed for the king inside the
church, and then takes him outside of the place of reception and to the door
of entrance. Up to this point the people carrying candles are encouraged by
the sung texts and the ceremony to identify with Mary who, accompanied
by Joseph her husband, brought Jesus to the Temple. Then the announcement that he is coming is made through the station in front of the major
portal of the church.

This ceremony makes the cathedral of Chartres a type of the Temple
of Jerusalem, and of its transformation by the coming of the Messiah into
the Church. We should note, by way of contrast, that none of the other
major processions of the church year at Chartres were internal processions
(although many lesser ones were); all the other major processions had stations
at other churches. This Purification procession was unique because it was
in honor of the Virgin; hence the crowd, led by the bishop and his clergy,
processes *from* her church and then directly *back into* her church, making a
station at their own church! The point would have been made powerfully
and dramatically for every citizen in the town, as the major processions were
important civic as well as religious events.

In front of the door the bishop prayed the ancient "Erudi quesumus
domine plebem tuam" proper to the feast, which asks that the outer meaning of the ceremony be directed inward by "the light of divine grace," this

being a reference to the candles.[53] The bishop then offered the traditional blessing, which begins "Sit nomen domini benedictum," and everyone, having been blessed, processed inside. The crowd then moved forward to the front of the nave, and there another station was made before the cross on the *jubé*. The Gospel book, which would have been part of the procession, was returned to its place within the church; it would seem that on occasions when the bishop was present the book was returned to a lectern on top of the *jubé,* from where the bishop may have offered a sermon to the people. A short sermon for the feast survives, attributed to Bishop Fulbert.[54] The excerpt below is Fulbert's gloss upon the meaning of the candles in relation to the sense of the feast as celebrated in Chartres Cathedral in the early eleventh century:

> But this presentation was glorious and specially marked: moved by the Holy Spirit, the holy prophet Symeon and the holy widow and prophetess Anna met him, praising and blessing the Lord for the *Adventus Christi,* just as is said in the Gospel, predicting miraculous things. For Christ, as he came in the flesh, brothers, displayed both an example of humility and the signs of divine love. As at his nativity, when he lay humbly in the crib, he was celebrated in the heavens by a new star and the praises of the angels, so in like manner, as the tiny infant was presented in the Temple, the Holy Spirit illuminated the hearts of the prophets to declare his divinity concealed in the flesh. We therefore, who adore in memory of his presentation in the Temple the one who is both true God and true human being, celebrate this day with an oblation of candles: expressing divinity through the light of the candle, and his virginal flesh through the wax. The bee is the creator both of sweet honey and of wax, which are made without intercourse of male and female. Therefore it is evident that at the presentation of Christ he processed into the Temple out of obedience to the Law, and our oblation derives its significance from the sweet and venerable remembrance of his presentation.[55]

The bishop's words explain the meaning of the historical event and of the community's reenactment of the event. History was remade in liturgy through communal memory; this depended not only upon ceremony and upon tangible objects that are theologically significant, but also upon the teachers who explained what the things meant and how the physical re-enactment stood between both past events and present action. Here, as in all medieval *memoria,* the outer signs exist on several levels, the most important being the inner spiritual state of the persons involved in the commemoration. Historical events were reenacted within communities not only to rediscover the past, but also to inspire living individuals in intimately personal ways. The candles signified a Messiah who is both divine and human: those carrying the candles remembered an event from the Bible, while at the same time they proclaimed a theological understanding central to the Christian mystery. Just as throughout the Middle Ages the learned were taught to read scripture on several levels, so too the learned *and* the unlettered were taught to understand liturgical events from multiple perspectives, one of which was always to find a place for themselves in the re-created sense of the past offered by the *adventus* ceremony adapted for the Feast of the Purification.

The Palm Sunday Procession: Entering Jerusalem

The second major procession of the medieval church year, in Chartres as elsewhere, was that of Palm Sunday. Although it is the most studied of all medieval processions, it has not been analyzed specifically as an *adventus* ceremony, with attention to the texts of the chants and to the readings in light of *adventus*.[56] Yet it surely was the most notable of all elaborate *adventus* ceremonies, a model with its major source in scripture, and it served to define royal processions throughout the Western world from the late antique period until long after the Middle Ages had come to an end. Here the cast of characters shifted from that assembled for the Purification. On Palm Sunday the bishop took on the role of Christ, the *populus* the role of the Hebrew people, and the clergy a variety of parts, depending upon immediate circumstances. The topography of the town, in Chartres and in other cities of northern Europe, was used deliberately to remind all present that each city was, through liturgical action, a remade Jerusalem, and that the ancient rite observed by Egeria in the place where it actually occurred had been transported everywhere.[57]

As was the case in the Feast of the Purification, the chants and readings define the action; the action in turn makes the sense of chants and texts obvious even to those who might not have understood the Latin of the texts. The texts of the Bible, in their turn, existed in the medieval imagination against the background not only of liturgical proclamation but also of liturgical reenactment. On Palm Sunday, perhaps with more detail than on any other day, the liturgy of the morning Office was drawn out from the confines of the choir and restated dramatically; thus all the people had a role, and through their participation gained comprehension of historical events depicted in the Bible and their theological interpretation.

The nun Egeria's description of the feast as celebrated in fourth-century Jerusalem was not essentially different from the dramatic service that inspired Western pilgrims to the city for centuries after her death, and which they took back home with them.[58] The basic shape of the procession has been much studied and is well understood.[59] In the Middle Ages, all the people— clergy, laity, and saints—transported Christ (in the person of the bishop) from the Mount of Olives down into the city of Jerusalem, to the Anastasis, the church built on the cave of the tomb.[60] Although clearly an *adventus Christi,* nonetheless the Palm Sunday procession differed in character from every other: although celebrated outwardly with waving branches of victory and festive displays that looked forward to the triumph of Easter, the throngs accompanied the King more immediately to his death. The message of the celebration was not only that he would die for them, but also that the guilt for the killing was their own. Bright and clear though the day might have been, the liturgy created a powerful undertow of remorse. At Chartres the joy was undercut in a variety of ways as the clergy, garbed in red robes to mark the blood of the passion, prepared to lead their Master to the ceremonial betrayal of Holy Week.

The liturgical books of Chartres, those of the cathedral and of the other churches, allow the study of the rite from multiple perspectives.[61] The ordinals, books that list the particular chants and readings of the entire church year, are extant in multiple copies, as can be seen in Table 2 in the appendix.[62] Although the most dramatic events of the procession were observed by the assembled town, Palm Sunday began normally enough with Matins and Lauds in each individual church. Thus all clergy, secular and Benedictine, would have heard readings proper to the day from the Lamentations of the Prophet Jeremiah and selections from Pope Leo I and from Ambrose's commentary on Luke, book 9, an excerpt from which must be quoted here, for it helps explain certain aspects of the ceremony later in the day:

> Beautifully does the Lord, having left the Jews and being about to take up his abode in the hearts of the Gentiles, go up to the Temple. This is the true Temple in which he is worshipped not in the letter but in the spirit, God's Temple whose foundations are laid not in stone but in faith. He leaves behind those who hate him, and chooses those who will love him. And therefore he comes to the Mount of Olives that he may plant on the heights of virtue the young olive branches whose mother is the Jerusalem that is above. On this mountain is he, the heavenly husbandman, that all who have been planted in the House of God may be able to say: "I am like a fruitful olive-tree in the House of God" (Ps. 51:10).[63]

The responsories punctuating the readings from the Lamentations, Leo, and Ambrose emphasize themes of royalty forsaken and abandoned, of goodness repaid by evil and persecution. The abandoned King cries out in these chants for help from God, offering lamentations to parallel those of Jeremiah, who chastised the people, calling them harlots with poor memories who forgot that they had been "a noble vine, wholly a right seed" (themes also found in Ambrose in the excerpt above). The procession of clergy and people from the cathedral was organized amid a massive peal of bells, and prominent within the carefully ordered assembly was the *capsa,* the term used in the Chartrain ordinals for the major relic of the cathedral in its reliquary.[64] The presence of the major relic of the church is crucial for understanding the special character of the procession at Chartres, for through its presence Mary walks with her son during the beginning of his most difficult journey.

The chapter and the bishop set out to join the processions of all the other churches. The responsories of the morning Office were sung this time out of doors in the midst of the people—all save one, that is, the responsory *Ingrediente,* which was deliberately left out of the accustomed line-up, reserved for singing at a particular point later in the day. The churches, their clergy and relics and people, converged on one spot, the cemetery of St. Bartholomew. There the common reenactment of Christ's entry into Jerusalem began with the singing of the responsory *Circumdederunt*. The chant text encourages a multiplicity of meanings: based on Psalm 3, it puts the words of David in the mouth of Christ, proclaiming his lineage; based on the scourging scene from the Gospel of Matthew as well, it also looks forward to the proclamation of Christ as King of the Jews, and his martyrdom. Those who sing are associated with the King about to die; those who process with him are both his subjects and his killers. Sung with its customary repeats, and without the Gloria, the text is rendered as follows:

> Liars surround me, they have fallen upon me with scourges without a cause. Do you Lord, O my Redeemer, avenge me. [Verse] For trouble is near, and there is none to help. [Repetition] Do you Lord, O my Redeemer, avenge me. Liars surround me, they have fallen upon me with scourges without a cause. Do you Lord, O my Redeemer, avenge me.

The procession of all the churches then moved out to the hill of St. Cheron, again singing responsories from the morning Office, heard now for the third time. Upon entering the Church of St. Cheron, songs of glory and honor were solemnly sung and the hour of Terce offered, followed by the ceremonial leaving of the church. At this point the singing of music marked by "Hosanna" began, and the palms and other floral branches, blessed during the singing of Terce, were distributed to the people.[65] With the people thus transformed into Jews of the time of Christ, a constant alternation between acknowledgment and betrayal informed the character of the crowd. The procession left St. Cheron to the murmuring text of the processional antiphon *Collegerunt,* which (according to the *Ordo veridicus*), with its several verses, was long enough to get the procession back to the cross. This was apparently in the cemetery of St. Bartholomew, where earlier the several processions had joined together; this place in the suburbs was known for its location at the fork in the road on the way to St. Cheron, and for its cross "in the atrium," which Paul of St. Père mentions as a distinctive marker.[66] Who would betray the King, why, and when? The text of the long chant accompanying the march back to the cross of Bartholomew's is a pastiche of verses from John 11:47–51, all of which could be repeated for as long as was necessary for the action to be completed:

The chief priests therefore, and the Pharisees, gathered a council, and said: What do we, for this man doth many miracles? If we leave him alone so, all will believe in him; and the Romans will come and take away our place and nation. But one of them, named Caiphas, being the high priest that year, prophesied to them saying: it is expedient for you that one man should die for the people, and that the whole people not perish. From that day forward they devised to put him to death.

In the cemetery children and youths were separated from the bishop, the processional crosses, reliquaries, and the people; in the voices of the Hebrew children they acknowledged the Ruler with an antiphonal public singing of the famous Carolingian hymn, "Gloria laus et honor." In this text the King is hailed and his identity is acknowledged; at the same time the historical event is recapitulated, and the present event is related to it in the language and gestures of court ceremonial from the time of Charlemagne. In an *adventus* ceremony, announcement must be made of identity: Who is this King? How do we know he is King? The text supplies a great number of answers:

(Opening and Refrain, sung between the verses) Glory and praise to you, Christ, Redeemer King: To whom children pour out their glad hosannas.

Hail, Israel's King! Hail, David's Son confessed! who comes in the name of Israel's Lord.

The angelic host sings your praise in heaven; on earth humankind, with all created things.

Once the Jews went forth to meet you with palms; now we greet you with prayers and holy hymns.

As you were on your way to die they crowned you with praise; now to you, King on high, we raise our melody.

These pleased you; may our devotion please you; O good King, O wise King, whom an abundance of good things please.

The next part of the ceremony was surely one of the most dramatic and compelling of the entire day, for here the community defined itself even more specifically. The King had been proclaimed and twice recognized by the historic persons represented by the Chartrain crowd. But who were the members of that crowd? The crowd's dual nature has been steadily defined, beginning in the Office liturgy of the day with the reading from Ambrose. The singing of the antiphon *Occurrunt* brings the crowd to a deciding point, a ritual of public supplication before the Ruler, who is here represented by the symbol of his kingdom, the cross.

Several sets of rubrics for the performance of the ritual are extant. *Châteaudun 13*, the now missing manuscript that contained the twelfth-century ordinal, also contained an early *rituale* from around the year 1200; it provided rubrics for this ceremony very similar to those found in *Chartres Bibliothèque Municipale 520*, but apparently slightly earlier.[67] The antiphon was first intoned by either the bishop or the cantor, and he and the people with him prostrated themselves on the words "Filium Dei"; subsequently the antiphon was intoned by the succentor, and he and the singers with him prostrated themselves on the words "Filium Dei"; for a third time the antiphon was intoned, by the bishop or the cantor, and prostration was made as before. (Thus the bishop/cantor section of the choir prostrated itself twice, and the succentor's section once.) The melody of the antiphon is very simple, the music lending itself well to this athletic performance.

> Occurrunt turbae cum floribus et palmis Redemptori obviam: et victori triumphanti digna dant obsequia: Filium Dei ore gentes praedicant: et in laudem Christi voces tonant per nubila: Hosanna!

> ----

> [The multitude goes out to meet the Redeemer with flowers and palms, and pays the homage due to a triumphant conqueror: the nations proclaim the Son of God, and their voices thunder in praise of Christ through the skies: Hosanna!]

Following this triple prostration the antiphon *Turba multa* was sung, and the bishop preached a sermon. Complaints were heard from those who had them. Those who were to be excommunicated were officially separated from the worshipping body of the church.[68] A sermon of Ivo of Chartres interprets the ceremony and its complex meaning, which allowed each participant to become more fully engaged with his or her role in the communal drama. The work demonstrates the character of an early twelfth-century sermon for this occasion, revealing Ivo as a public liturgical commentator and teacher of the clergy and people, a man who believed in the importance of public ritual to instruct all members of his flock concerning theological truths.

> Such are these running up today to the Lord coming to the place of his passion: they see a humble person sitting on a donkey, yet nonetheless they show him triumphant and glorious by carrying branches of trees, and, spreading them out in the road, they sing imperial praises to him, because with the prophetic spirit they know him to be the giver of life, and triumphant over death and the devil. Dear brothers, you reproduce the form of this multitude, when you carry green branches of trees in your hands following the standard of the holy cross. And well you represent if what is signified by greenery in your hands, ever may it be kept in your way of life, and not die in the winter nor wither in the summer. . . . Christ humbled himself for us; let us humble ourselves for him.[69]

The people entered the gates of the city, purged for a time of their earlier guilt; they have acknowledged the Lord ceremonially, and those who do not belong (those with extraordinary sins, the heretics, and the Jews) have been formally separated from their company. Even those not part of the company are actors in the design. The long-awaited responsory *Ingrediente* describes "Hebrew children" (traditional translation) who know that the Lord will rise from the dead:

> When the Lord entered the holy city, the Hebrew children, pronouncing his resurrection, cried "Hosanna in the highest" with branches of palms.

The procession marched into the cathedral led by seven lighted candles and the *capsa* containing the Holy Chemise (Chartres' most precious relic) was replaced on the altar, uncovered, for adoration all the rest of the day.

The complex duality of the Palm Sunday procession has to do with the history of the ceremony in the West as well as with the nature of liturgical observance in Chartres Cathedral. As study of the homiliaries catalogued by Reginald Grégoire reveals, "Palm Sunday" was not a feature of the earliest layers of Roman liturgical sources.[70] Early Roman homiliaries have a ceremony for the palms as a vigil service after the last Sunday in Lent. By the time of Paul the Deacon's homiliary, compiled in the late eighth century, there is a Sunday for the Passion, followed by Palm Sunday, a liturgical plan that was carried everywhere that the Carolingian liturgical reforms took root. The texts of the Mass liturgy as sung in Chartres and elsewhere are passion texts, however, and have nothing to do with the ceremony of the palms and the entrance into Jerusalem.[71] The *adventus* procession and its many standardized texts shaped the popular character of the feast.

The Ascension Procession: Entering the Heavenly Kingdom

The third major procession of the church year took place on the Feast of the Ascension, which fell after a long, three-day rogation procession through the town.[72] As the rogation processions were situated in late spring, the first fruits from the fields were already visible, and the agrarian society received a blessing, parish by parish, for the long summer stretching ahead. Ascension was a culminating point, not only of the entire temporal cycle, but also of the work of preparing the land for planting, for getting seeds and plants in the ground, and for pleading with God for his help in feeding the community. On Ascension, with the days of supplication having passed, the community celebrated victory over sin and death, and over winter and hunger. The Feast of the Ascension is little discussed by scholars, yet at Chartres and other northern European towns it was marked by a dramatic event, an *adventus* ceremony in which the people themselves got to play the part of the conqueror's troops and to display his captured prey.

Here, too, the *adventus* themes associated with the elaborate procession are proclaimed in the chant texts that accompany the action. The procession is less extensive and detailed than that of Palm Sunday, but the sources suggest that all the churches—or at least those most directly affiliated—marched to the cathedral. It was ordered with candles, processional crosses, and Gospel books, but at the front were the two distinct features that marked this processional march: festive banners and the dragon. The beast would have made other appearances in processions during the post-Easter season, but this action was its last and most dramatic until the following year.[73]

The first responsory to accompany the procession was the one that opened the morning Office:

> After his passion, he appeared to them for forty days, speaking of the kingdom of God, Alleluia; and he was lifted up as they watched, and the clouds took him from their sight, Alleluia.

The procession was to the Church of St. Aniane (Aignan, an early bishop of Chartres), a short mile from the cathedral; this was not a long procession, and it took place in the very heart of the city. This was the parish church near to the castle of the Count of Chartres/Blois; associating the feast and its celebration with this particular church was a way of praising the local leader and his military might. The ordinal is specific: the processional music to be sung on the return to the cathedral from St. Aniane was to begin just as the people left the doorway of St. Aniane, and they were to sing it all the way to the cathedral. This music, which explained the sense of the action and of the feast, was the great Carolingian sequence, to be heard again later in the day during the Mass liturgy, "Rex omnipotens." This famous chant was performed on the Ascension throughout Europe; it acknowledges the entrance of the triumphant King to his heavenly throne.[74] We may imagine that in the twelfth century it would have been sung antiphonally, with two choirs alternating the half strophes:[75]

> On this day the all-powerful King, having redeemed the world by his triumphant power, ascended to heaven from whence he had descended.

> For forty days after he rose from the dead, strengthening in these holy days the minds of the apostles, he left dear kisses of peace to those to whom he gave the power of forgiving sins; and he sent them into the world to baptize all souls in the clemency of the Father, the Son, and the Holy Spirit.

> And turning back he commanded them not to leave Jerusalem, but to await the promised gift. "After not many days I will send to you on

earth the Spirit Paraclete, and you will be my witnesses in Jerusalem, in Judea, and in Samaria."

When he had said this, as they were watching he was lifted up and a bright cloud took him from before their eyes; as they were looking in the air

Behold, two men clothed in white appeared nearby saying, "What do you wonder at in the high heavens?

"This Jesus, who has been taken up from you to the right hand of the Father,

As he ascended, so will he come seeking increase from the money he entrusted to you."

O God of the sea, of the stars, of the land, the human creature whom you created, whom with sly deceit the enemy expelled from paradise and dragged with himself captive into Hell,

Whom you redeemed by your own blood for God: when you come as Judge to judge the world, you will raise [him] there whence the first joys of paradise were made corrupt.

Give us, we beg, perpetual rest in the homeland of the saints,

In which we all will sing to you "Alleluia."[76]

This *adventus* is for a King who has triumphed, but who has left his kingdom, arranging things so that it will be rightfully ruled until he returns, as he promises to do. The kingdom he has left behind is far different from when he first came to it: its enemies have been defrauded and slain; the lives of all its subjects have been transformed. At Chartres, the procession entered the cathedral singing of triumph and displaying the captured prey that had been marched through the town throughout the prior three days, and earlier as well. They nailed the massive dragon up high on the *jubé*—the first of which was built by Ivo of Chartres in the early twelfth century. This particular part of the ceremony must date at least from his time. The power of the dragon's image in the Chartrain imagination is revealed in the marginalia of a twelfth-century liturgical book from the cathedral where a robust dragon is shown decorating a sermon from the season on one folio, while on another he is upside down. The sketch may suggest what the Chartrain dragon looked like in the twelfth century.[77]

Looking up, the "men of Galilee" heard the Gospel read from the pulpit above a cloud of dragon, with the heels of the speaker treading on the head of sin and death. Ivo of Chartres explained the sense:

> Today, brothers, the victory of Christ was completed; today his triumphant banners are raised on high: Hell grieves with its ruler over lost plunder; the army of heaven rejoices over the restoration of its condemned. Today the flesh that was raised up from the earth was gathered to the right hand of the Father; so it was displayed to all creation and every commander and authority bowed before it. Today the "new way" of which the Apostle Paul spoke was consecrated for us, because through the flesh of Christ the door of heaven through which no flesh previously had gone was unlocked. And this "way" is living to this day just as the Apostle says, because in his time it was made ready for the members of Christ about to enter through it.[78] Today too the solemn opening of the book was completed, which no one was able to open except the Lamb who was slain. Formerly his sacraments were revealed by things found about Christ in the law and the prophets; today, with the dispensation of his humanity consummated, they are fulfilled. First Christ came down so that he might be made a participant in our nature; afterwards he ascended, so that he might make us participants in his glory; descending, with temporary intercourse and with visible miracles as if nursing babies; ascending he gave gifts to humankind. . . .

Central to Ivo's preaching is the idea that the hidden mysteries of the Old Testament are consummated and revealed by the messianic oracles of the Gospels, and liturgical feasts proclaim the meanings of both so they can be made alive again to those present.[79] Here, then, is yet another way in which the meaning of several layers of scripture resounded at once within ceremonial reenactment. The banners, and the slain and evil captive, framed the joy of subjects whose kingdom had been preserved by a Ruler willing to offer himself for their well-being; this Ruler had been hailed in the Old Testament and in the Gospels, and is the same one who is being hailed on Ascension Day. For centuries, the ideal of the good king was continually defined in public liturgies such as the *adventus* of Ascension Day. Although rightful rule might be lacking in the secular kingdom, the ideal was ever present, both to sustain the people in hard times and to offer hope for the future.

Conclusion: *Adventus* and the Twelfth-Century Royal Portal at Chartres

Medieval perceptions of power and its exercise were conditioned by the ongoing liturgical ceremonies that have just been described, each of which took place in Chartres—and in cathedral towns throughout Europe every year. The fact that by at least the twelfth century all Western Christians were shaped by these public displays of welcome and acknowledgment goes a long way to explaining the musical, dramatic, and visual arts of the period. Each liturgical *adventus*—from the ceremonial entrance at an episcopal Mass to the Palm Sunday and Ascension processions—was distinct; yet each was also part of a symbolic liturgical language that was spoken and comprehended to varying degrees by all members of the celebrating community, and even to those who chose not to celebrate. As Coulet has demonstrated, the ceremonies and their processions were increasingly difficult for the Jewish populations of medieval Europe: proclamations of history and faith traditions worked increasingly to ostracize them and even to humiliate and harm them.[80] The ceremonies described here could be used as a framework for destruction as well as for increasing a sense of identity and well-being.[81]

Ecclesial power represented in *adventus* and its processions was defined by those who standardized the liturgy and who were engaged throughout the twelfth century in Chartres in a massive building campaign. The processions of Chartres depended upon houses of Canons Regular, most of whom were either founded or reformed by the twelfth-century's two most powerful bishops, Ivo of Chartres and Geoffrey of Lèves, both of whom were great builders. The first Chartrain ordinal (OV) was apparently put together in the

FIGURE 1. The west portal—the "Royal Portal." Photo courtesy of Henri de Feraudy.

first half of the twelfth century, under the sway of these two leaders, both of whom had hopes of reforming the cathedral canons as well. The processions outlined in the Chartrain ordinals allow for the domination of the cathedral canons and the Augustinian churches, often at the expense of the Benedictine Abbey of St. Père and those few churches dependent upon it. The processions viewed here have a dramatic teaching agenda as well as a reforming agenda, and both were entwined in the ideals of the Canons Regular in the twelfth century.[82]

We should not be surprised, then, that the art of the West Portal of Chartres Cathedral (fig. 1) is dependent upon the dramatic portrayal of *adventus* found in the major processions of the church year, and it is only fitting to conclude this discussion through a brief look at the Royal Portal, a work that is filled with themes related to *adventus* (as, of course, is all portal sculpture from the period). Most generally, the jamb statues, originally twenty-four in number, are clustered around the three doors in the portal to receive processions. The themes of portal iconography are traditionally taken from the liturgy of the Advent season and also embody texts from Revelation, to make the parallel between Christ's first and second comings.[83] *Adventus Christi* ceremonies focus both on birth and renewal, but in a cosmic sense as the coming and going across boundaries of time. The jamb statues represent the figures before Christ who were his ancestors, not only as king, but also as priest and prophet.[84] But they—the kings, queens, and priests—are clad in the dress of twelfth-century figures and would have been immediately recognized as such by people in the twelfth century.[85] In this interpretation of *adventus,* the royal, priestly, and prophetic party stands at the door, ready to greet the new king. But they are frozen and silent, a contrast to the joyful *adventus* ceremonies described here. Unlike those in the procession, they seem not to be able to enter the building, but rather remain a people left behind (fig. 2).

There are other allusions to *adventus* found in the portal sculpture beside the most prominent ones embodied in the jambs. The invisible Christ of the liturgical processions studied here is made visible in his comings and goings through visual arts that depict his earthly actions, sometimes with deliberate multi-layered design. The northern tympanum (fig. 3) refers to his coming in the season of Advent as well as his leaving the earth at the Ascension. In this depiction, the apostles see him off, but in a design that suggests their counterparts, the prophets who originally awaited him (fig. 4).[86] As the sequence sung before the portal in the twelfth century "Rex omnipotens" states, he returns from whence he came. The line of disciples are not the only figures who watch the king enter his kingdom; he is also hailed by angels who are especially vigorous in their praise, offering voice with open mouths that sing of joy at this entrance. They help us imagine the stance and liveliness of medieval choristers who sang songs of welcome in twelfth-century ceremonies of *adventus,* for they depict the ideal especially desired by medieval cantors and those they trained.

Yet other *adventus* formulae can be seen in the southern tympanum that is dedicated to the Virgin Mary. On the first lintel, the shepherds and angels herald the newborn king who has come into the world of time and who lies in a basket above his pensive mother (fig. 5). In the lintel just above, this breadbasket babe has been transferred to the altar in the Temple in Jerusalem, where he is presented by his mother and received by the prophet Symeon. The first purification feast depicted here is characterized by a procession as well, as the Virgin's relatives and friends bring the characteristic gifts of doves as they accompany the king to his formal reception. Here, as on the northern tympanum, models of *adventus* inform the processions that actually took place in twelfth-century Chartres, this with reference to the Purification,

FIGURE 2.   The Royal Portal, southern door, right splay. Photo courtesy of Henri de Feraudy.

FIGURE 3.   The Royal Portal, northern tympanum. Photo courtesy of Henri de Feraudy.

FIGURE 4.   The Royal Portal, northern door, lintel. Photo courtesy of Henri de
Feraudy.

FIGURE 5.   The Royal Portal, southern tympanum. Photo courtesy of Henri de
Feraudy.

FIGURE 6.   The Royal Portal, central tympanum. Photo courtesy of Henri de Feraudy.

whose procession halted before this door and was defined and refined by the artwork.

The central tympanum (fig. 6) is the most important and widespread *adventus* iconography of the twelfth century, and refers to the hailing of the King at the end of time as found in Revelation. He pushes through from the east, with the sun at his back, accompanied by the four mystical creatures who represent the evangelists in traditional Christian exegesis: "Behold, he cometh with the clouds, and every eye shall see him, and they also that pierced him, and all the tribes of the earth shall bewail themselves because of him" (Rev. 1: 7); and all of chapter 4 of this book which explains the entourage of the enthroned King. The texts quoted here were used extensively for the Feast of Holy Innocents, December 28, the day on which the acolytes were especially honored. Revelation 1:8, "I am Alpha and Omega, the beginning the end, saith the Lord God, who is, and who was, and who is to come, the Almighty," formed the text of an antiphon featured in the Chartrain liturgy for processions through the weeks just after Easter.[87] Also the book was read in the Office liturgy in the weeks immediately following

Easter, this too giving prominence to the text.[88] The heralding of this king will take place in the future, and the depiction of a future *adventus* contains a warning. Angels come with a crown not yet on his head (figs. 7 and 8).

The southern tympanum celebrates the eternal coming of the Messiah, with a powerful allusion to the Purification. The northern tympanum can be read as an *adventus Domini* and as an Ascension scene.[89] The Christ in majesty in the center tympanum is depicted at his Second Coming. All three represent ideals of the *adventus* ceremony and make the Royal Portal a backdrop for the action of the liturgy and a framework for processions of all types, but most specifically for those of the Ascension and the Purification. The Palm Sunday procession featured an *adventus* and splendid entrance, but it was depicted only on the capital frieze (figs. 9 and 10). The Royal Portal was the primary door of a church dedicated to the Virgin and to mysteries associated with incarnation and birth. Throughout the Middle Ages, *adventus* had a form, a set of formulae, and an easily recognizable mode of action. But all these things, as at Chartres, were modified in accordance with local cults and interpretations of history. To understand *adventus* is the first step toward developing sensitivity to these details and finding within them the footprints of those who marched through the portals of the past.

APPENDIX

Table 1. Processions at Chartres in the Twelfth and Thirteenth Centuries

I. Processions within and around the Cathedral of Notre Dame
    A. "Ferial" procession before Terce out of the choir, either within or outside the church, with a station in front of the cross on the *jubé*.
    B. Sunday processions before Terce.
    C. Entrance processions of the Bishop.
    D. Processions before the Gospel at Mass on major feast days.
    E. Processions before Vespers within the cathedral.
    F. Processions during the Octave of Christmas.
        1. The Feast of St. Stephen (Dec. 26), the procession of the deacons.
        2. The Feast of St. John the Evangelist (Dec. 27), the procession of the priests.
        3. The Feast of the Holy Innocents (Dec. 28), the procession of the boys.
        4. The Feast of the Circumcision (Jan. 1), the feast of the subdeacons.

FIGURE 7. Archivolt, central door (detail). Photo courtesy of Henri de Feraudy.

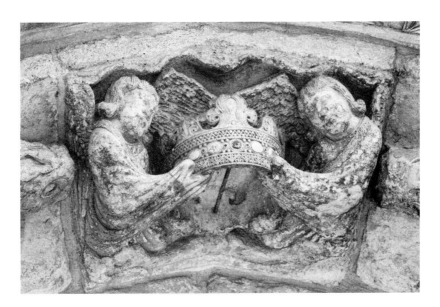

FIGURE 8. Archivolt, central door (detail). Photo courtesy of Henri de Feraudy.

FIGURE 9. The Royal Portal, southern door, frieze (detail). Photo courtesy of Henri de Feraudy.

FIGURE 10. The Royal Portal, southern door, frieze (detail). Photo courtesy of Henri de Feraudy.

G. Christmas and Epiphany. At Matins, the ninth responsory was sung twice while the deacon processed into the *jubé* from whence he proclaimed the genealogy of Christ.
H. The Purification (February 2).
I. Ash Wednesday. The ejection of the penitents.
J. Processions during Vespers of Easter week.
K. Vigil of Pentecost: Blessing of the fonts.

II. External Processions
    A. Lenten Stational Liturgy.

Week 1:	Monday:	St. Stephen
	Wednesday:	St. Saturninus
	Friday:	St. John in the Valley
Week 2:	Monday:	St. Maurice
	Wednesday:	St. Andrew
	Friday:	St. Bartholomew and St. Cheron
Week 3:	Monday:	St. Michael
	Wednesday:	St Peter in the Valley (St.-Père)
	Friday:	St. Martin in the Valley
Week 4:	Monday:	St. John in the Valley; St. Maurice
	Wednesday	St. Andrew
	Friday:	St. Bartholomew and St. Cheron
Week 5:	Monday:	St. Aniane
	Wednesday:	St. Peter in the Valley (St. Père)
	Friday:	St. Martin in the Valley

    B. Palm Sunday
      1. *Collectio* ceremony at the cathedral
      2. Procession to the cemetery of St. Bartholomew.
      3. Procession to St. Cheron for Terce and the blessing and distribution of the palms.
      4. Procession back to the Porte Cendreuse.
      5. Singing of the response "Ingrediente Domino in sanctam civitatem."
      6. Terce and Mass at the cathedral.
    C. Stational Liturgy of Easter Week.
      1. Monday: St. Martin in the Valley
      2. Tuesday: St. Peter in the Valley (St. Père)
      3. Wednesday: St. John in the Valley
      4. Thursday: St. Andrew
      5. Friday: St. Maurice
    D. St. Mark (April 25): Procession with banners and the dragon to St. Peter in the Valley (St. Père)

E.   Rogations: three days before Ascension.
   1.   Monday: St. John in the Valley; St. Maurice;
                             St. Andrew
   2.   Tuesday: St. Bartholomew; St. Cheron;
                             St. Peter in the Valley (St. Père)
   3.   Wednesday: St. Michael; St. Martin; St. Lubin;
                             St. Saturninus; St. Faith
F.   Ascension: Procession to St. Aniane with the dragon for Terce. Return
     to the cathedral where the dragon was hung on the *jubé*.

Table 2. Selected Medieval Ordinals and Pontificals of Chartres

The table of processions was prepared using Chartrain ordinals surviving from
the twelfth and thirteenth centuries. The nature of the sources is complicated,
but taken as a group and supplemented with the rubrics from other sources—
primarily missals and antiphoners—they allow for the study of processional liturgy chiefly from two establishments: the Cathedral of Notre Dame, and the
Augustinian Abbey of St.-Jean-en-Vallée, which was reformed by Bishop Ivo of
Chartres in 1098.

1. *Châteaudun, Archive of the Hôtel Dieu 13,* which contains several books bound
together. The original is now missing, making codicological analysis impossible.
The first and most extensive portion—the *Ordo Veridicus* or OV—was copied
by Yves Delaporte and can be consulted in the Diocesan Archives of Notre Dame
de Chartres. The other portions are available in faint photographs that I tran-
scribed in preparation for this study.

> *Chât. 13 A,* the *Ordo Veridicus,* an ordinal from the mid-twelfth century, which
> reflects the use of Chartres Cathedral.

> *Chât. 13 B,* a truncated ordinal that contains the incipits for the Mass liturgy
> and appears to post-date the OV.

> *Chât. 13 C,* a sacramentary that dates from the early thirteenth century and
> that contains some rubrics.

2. *Chartres, Bibliothèque Municipale 1058* (the OC), which dates from the second
quarter of the thirteenth century. The original was destroyed in the fire of 1944,
but a microfilm copy survives. Yves Delaporte used this copy for his edition of
1953 (*L'ordinaire chartrain*).

3. *Paris, Bibliothèque Nationale lat. 1794.* This ordinal copied in the second half of
the twelfth century was prepared for the use of St. John in the Valley.

4. *Paris, Ste. Genevieve 1256*. This ordinal from the second half of the twelfth century was prepared for Notre Dame de Gâtins, a dependency of St. John in the Valley.

5. *Paris, Arsenal 838*. This fifteenth-century book has not been used for the present study.

6. *Paris, Bibliothèque Nationale lat. 945*. This pontifical from the late twelfth century was prepared for notation, but the neumes were not supplied.

7. *Orléans, Bibliothèque Municipale 144*. A fully notated Chartrain pontifical from the late twelfth century.

8. *Le Mans, Bibliothèque Municipale 432*. This pontifical is dated 1531.

NOTES

I am deeply grateful for the advice and help of Canon Pierre Bizeau, diocesan archivist of Chartres, for his permission to consult numerous materials and for his support during the many years I have worked on the liturgy of the cathedral. I am also indebted for the photographs and permission to publish them.

1. A much cited overview of the subject is Clifford Geertz, "Centers, Kings, and Charisma: Reflections on the Symbolics of Power," in *Culture and Its Creators: Essays in Honor of Edward Shils*, ed. Joseph Ben-David and Terry Nichols Clark (Chicago, 1977), 150–71. Broader concerns are addressed in Alfred van Gennep, *The Rites of Passage*, trans. Monika B. Vizedom and Gabrielle L Caffee (Chicago, 1960). Victor Turner's exploration of the "liminality" is found conveniently in *Readings in Ritual Studies*, ed. Ron Grimes (Upper Saddle River, 1996), 511–19.

2. See Noël Coulet, "De l'intégration à l'exclusion: la place des juifs dans les cérémonies d'entrée solennelle au Moyen Ages," *Annales* 34 (1979): 662–83.

3. See Bernard Guenée and Françoise Lehoux, *Les entrées royales françaises de 1328 à 1515* (Paris, 1968), with further reflection by Coulet in "Les entrées solennelles en Provence au XIVe siècles, aperçus nouveaux sur les entrées royales françaises au Bas Moyen Age," *Ethnologie française* 7 (1977): 63–82.

4. See Evelyne Patlagean, "L'entrée de la Sainte Face d'Edesse à Constantinople en 944," in *La religion civique à l'époque médiévale et moderne*, ed. André Vauchez (Rome, 1995).

5. Sible de Blaauw, "Contrasts in Processional Liturgy: A Typology of Outdoor Processions in Twelfth-Century Rome," in *Art, Cérémonial et Liturgie au Moyen Age*, ed. Nicholas Bock et al. (Rome, 2002), 357–94.

6. Processions have been much studied by students of ritual. See, for example, Ronald Grimes, *Symbol and Conquest: Public Ritual and Drama in Santa Fe*,

New Mexico (Ithaca, 1976). Students of the early modern period have a rich array of evidence to work with, as the bibliography assembled by Helen Watanabe-O'Kelly and Ann Simon attests: *Festivals and Ceremonies: A Bibliography of Works Relating to Court, Civic and Religious Festivals in Europe 1500–1800* (London, 2000). Much recent scholarship contains work on the place of the visual arts, music, and drama in processional contexts, e.g., Susan Verdi Webster, *Art and Ritual in Golden-Age Spain: Sevillian Confraternities and the Processional Sculpture of Holy Week* (Princeton, 1998), and Philine Helas, *Lebende Bilder in der italienischen Festkultur des 15. Jahrhunderts* (Berlin, 1999).

7. For recent studies demonstrating the great span of time during which the idea of *adventus* reigned, see, for imperial Rome, Joachim Lehnen, *Adventus principis: Untersuchungen zu Sinngehalt und Zeremoniell der Kaiserankunft in den Städten des Imperium Romanum* (Frankfurt am Main, 1997); for the late antique period, the collection *Imperial Art as Christian Art—Christian Art as Imperial Art: Expression and Meaning in Art and Architecture from Constantine to Justinian,* ed. J. Rasmus Brandt and Olaf Steen (Rome, 2001); for the early Middle Ages, M.-Fr. Auzepy, "Les déplacements de l'empereur dans la ville et ses environs (VIIIe–Xe siècles)" in *Constantinople and Its Hinterland,* ed. Cyril Mango et al. (Aldershot, 1995), 359–66; for the Carolingian period and central Middle Ages, David A. Warner, "Ritual and Memory in the Ottonian *Reich*: The Ceremony of *Adventus,*" *Speculum* 76 (2001): 255–83; for the twelfth century, Sible de Blaauw, "Contrasts in Processional Liturgy," and Maureen Miller, "The Florentine Bishop's Ritual Entry and the Origins of the Medieval Episcopal *Adventus,*" *Revue d'Histoire Ecclésiastique* 98 (2003): 5–28; and for the later Middle Ages, Gordon Kipling, *Enter the King: Theatre, Liturgy, and Ritual in the Medieval Civic Triumph* (Oxford, 1998).

8. "A vast crowd of citizens came out to meet him, carrying flags and banners, and singing songs in his praise. The speech of the Syrians contrasted sharply with that of those using Gallo-Roman and again with that of the Jews, as each sang his praises in his own tongue.'Long live the King!' they all shouted.'May he continue to reign over his peoples for more years that we can count!'" (*History of the Franks,* trans. Lewis Thorpe [London, 1974], 7.1.433). For an evaluation of Gregory of Tours on ritual, and a warning against interpreting descriptions of rites relating to kingship as mere portraits of the times, see Philippe Buc, *The Dangers of Ritual: Between Early Medieval Texts and Social Scientific Theory* (Princeton, 2001).

9. "Mounted on great Spanish steeds, they all go to meet the King of Britain, saluting King Arthur first with great courtesy and then all his company.'Welcome,' they say,'to this company, so full of honourable men! Blessed be he who brings them hither and presents us with such fair guests!' At the King's arrival the town resounds with the joyous welcome which they give. Silken stuffs are taken out and hung aloft as decorations, and they spread tapestries to walk upon and drape the streets with them, while they wait for the King's approach" (*Yvain,* in *Arthurian Romances,* trans. W. W. Comfort, Everyman's Library [London, 1914], Part 2.5, verse 2329 and following). For a brief introduction to Chrétien, see Renate Blumenfeld-

Kosinski, "Chrétien de Troyes as a Reader of the *Romans Antiques,*" *Philological Quarterly* 64 (1985): 398–405.

10. For a modern edition of this book and discussion of its sources, see Peter Dinter, ed., *Liber tramitis aevi Odilonis abbatis,* Corpus Consuetudinum Monasticarum 10 (Siegburg, 1980). For the liturgy of the Abbey of Farfa, with emphasis upon the period in which the customary was compiled, see Susan Boynton, *Shaping a Monastic Identity: Liturgy and History at the Imperial Abbey of Farfa, 1000–1125* (Ithaca, 2006). The similarities between various ceremonies of *Adventus* are demonstrated here. Following that for a king (and queen) is the ceremony for leading the bishop, and then the abbot, each with minor modifications.

11. Electronic searching of Office manuscripts for specific chants is now facilitated through *Cantus: A Database for Latin Ecclesiastical Chant,* founded by Ruth Steiner of the Catholic University of America; this on-line tool is now maintained by researchers at the University of Western Ontario. René-Jean Hesbert's *Corpus Antiphonalium Officii,* 6 vols. (Rome, 1963–1979) provides a catalogue of manuscript types from both monastic and cathedral uses and indices for both antiphons (commonly referring to short chants sung with intoned psalms) and responsories (more complex chants that featured the singing of soloists and that followed intoned readings from scripture, fathers, or saints' lives). Hesbert assigned each chant a number, now commonly called its "CAO number." For help in locating the scriptural sources of chants in the Roman rite, see Carl Marbach, *Carmina Scripturarum* (1907; repr. Hildesheim, 1994).

12. This antiphon is identified by Peter Dinter as CAO 2032 in Hesbert's *Corpus Antiphonalium Officii.* In any case the reference to Matthew 19:28 is clear.

13. The imagery of medieval *adventus* processions played a major role in later festive processions, as can be seen in Kipling, *Enter the King.*

14. The classic discussion of *adventus* and the visual arts in the antique and early medieval periods is Ernest Kantorowicz, "The 'King's Advent' and the Enigmatic Panels in the Doors of Santa Sabina," *Art Bulletin* 26 (1944): 207–31, reprinted in the author's *Selected Studies* (New York, 1965). For a survey of triumphant themes in medieval art, see Robert Baldwin, "I Slaughter Barbarians: Triumph as a Mode in Medieval Christian Art," in *Konsthistorisk Tidskrift* 59, no. 4 (1990): 225–42.

15. Displays of cruelty and death in medieval drama have strong links to this aspect of the *adventus.* For further reading on these themes, see especially the writings of Jody Enders: *Death by Drama and Other Medieval Urban Legends* (Chicago, 2002) and *Medieval Theater of Cruelty: Rhetoric, Memory, Violence* (Ithaca, 1999).

16. See Mary Ellen Miller, *The Murals of Bonampak* (Princeton, 1986). She suggests that the artists may themselves have been members of the vanquished group. Professor Miller has recently collaborated with contemporary artists to recreate a model of this striking work of art at Yale University.

17. See especially Michael McCormick, *Eternal Victory: Triumphal Rulership in Late Antiquity, Byzantium, and the Early Medieval West* (Cambridge, 1986).

18. For study of parallels between scenes from the New Testament, Roman practices, and later correspondences, see Pierre Dufraigne, *Adventus Augusti, Adventus Christi* (Paris, 1994).

19. On the politics of the play, see Cathy Shrank, "Civility and the City in *Coriolanus*," *Shakespeare Quarterly* 54 (2004): 406–23.

20. On the ways in which *adventus* ceremonies were used by popes as gestures of reconciliation, see Susan Tyman, "Papal *Adventus* at Rome in the Twelfth Century," *Historical Research* 69 (1996): 233–53.

21. Rodulfus Glaber, *The Five Books of the Histories,* trans. John France (Oxford, 1989), 1.23.41.

22. Suger, *The Deeds of Louis the Fat,* trans. Richard Cusimano and John Moorhead (Washington, D.C., 1992), 51–52.

23. For discussion of flaws within ritual practice and their meaning in the early medieval period, see Buc, *The Dangers of Ritual.*

24. See Ernst Kantorowicz, *"Laudes regiae": A Study in Liturgical Acclamations and Mediaeval Ruler Worship* (Berkeley, 1946); it includes a study of the music by Manfred Bukofzer. Anne Walters Robertson has demonstrated the ways in which the *laudes* of Reims were incorporated by Machaut into his strikingly resonant "David Hocket." See her *Guillaume de Machaut and Reims: Context and Meaning in His Musical Works* (Cambridge, 2002).

25. See my "The Feast of Fools and *Danielis Ludus*: Popular Tradition in a Medieval Cathedral Play," in *Plainsong in the Age of Polyphony,* ed. Thomas Kelly (Cambridge, 1992), 65–99.

26. The discussion of the medieval Feast of Fools has a vast bibliography, summarized in Fassler, "The Feast of Fools and *Danielis Ludus*," and in Wulf Arlt, "The Office for the Feast of the Circumcision from Le Puy," in *The Divine Office in the Latin Middle Ages,* ed. Margot E. Fassler and Rebecca A. Baltzer (Oxford, 2000), 324–43. The most detailed early study is in E. K. Chambers, *The Drama of the Mediaeval Church;* Michel Foucault's *Madness and Civilization* (first published in French in 1961, but revised by the author for the English translation by Richard Howard, 1967) is the most influential modern critical study of the social role of "the fool."

27. See my "The Feast of Fools and *Danielis Ludus*," 89–92, for full discussion.

28. As the table shows, the medieval cathedral liturgy as celebrated in Chartres was strongly marked by processions, inside the church, to its immediate environs, and throughout the town and outlying regions. Some of these processions were dominated by personnel from the cathedral; others involved the cathedral clergy with the clergy and monks of other churches; still others depended directly upon the *populus* to achieve their intentions. Clearly every region of the town was bound to every other through these processions, and the church and its patron saints offered a sense of identity that was held up and celebrated: every corner of the town had days of special importance, when attention was offered by the whole to the discrete part.

29. Much of the evidence for this essay, especially that for the Palm Sunday procession, was laid out in two papers, one given at the national meeting of the American Musicological Society in Vancouver in 1985, and the second in a discussion of the processions of Chartres Cathedral in New Brunswick, New Jersey, in 1995, at a conference organized by Professor Karl Morrison. I offer thanks to the Griswold Fund of Yale University for support in developing a collection of Chartrain liturgical books on microfilm. Michael Powell's M.A. thesis, "Spacial Considerations in Liturgy: The Palm Sunday Procession at Chartres" (Yale Institute of Sacred Music, 1988), used Chartrain liturgical materials to discuss the concept of *civitas* in the Middle Ages.

30. The ecclesial politics underlying Chartrain processions in the twelfth century is discussed in my *Making History: The Virgin of Chartres and the Liturgical Framework of Time* (New Haven, 2007).

31. As can be seen in *Making History,* the ways the sculptures were arranged at Chartres were influenced by liturgical practices.

32. For comparison of the general outline of the Palm Sunday procession at Chartres to those of ten other northern French cathedrals, see Craig Wright, "The Palm Sunday Procession in Medieval Chartres," in *The Divine Office in the Latin Middle Ages,* ed. Margot E. Fassler and Rebecca A. Baltzer (Oxford, 2000), 361–64.

33. See *Making History,* chapter 3.

34. New texts, newly composed or adapted chants, and ceremonies of several types from around the year 1000 abound, and significant numbers of these served to proclaim *adventus* of one sort or another. Especially relevant here are the introit trope repertories, for which see my "Liturgy and Sacred History in the Twelfth-Century Tympana at Chartres," *The Art Bulletin* 75 (1993): 499–520, and "The Meaning of Entrance: Liturgical Commentaries and the Introit Tropes," in *Reflections on the Sacred: A Musicological Perspective,* ed. Paul Brainard (New Haven, 1994), 8–18, as well as David Hiley, "Provins, Bibliothèque Municipale 12 (24), a Thirteenth-Century Gradual with Tropes from Chartres Cathedral," in *Recherches nouvelles sur les tropes liturgiques: recueil d'études,* ed. W. Arlt and G. Björkvall (Stockholm, 1993), and Wulf Arlt, "Zu Einigen Fragen der Funktion, Interpretation und Edition der Introitustropen," in *Referate zweier Colloquium des Corpus Troporum in München und Canterbury* (Munich, 1985), 131–50.

35. For the Gospel procession, see Anne Walters Robertson, "From Office to Mass: The Antiphons of Vespers and Lauds and the Antiphons before the Gospel in Northern France," in *The Divine Office in the Latin Middle Ages,* ed. Margot E. Fassler and Rebecca A. Baltzer (Oxford, 2000), 300–23.

36. On the power of *Adventus* to re-create the past and modify understandings of history, see especially Warner, "Ritual and Memory."

37. For an overview of the centrality of liturgy to the medieval process of re-creating the past, see my *Making History,* chapter 1. This chapter was given as a plenary address at the International Medieval Conference at Kalamazoo, 2004, and I

am grateful to Paul Szarmach for his support and to Richard Emmerson of the Medieval Academy of America that sponsored the address.

38. This idea is discussed at length in *Making History,* chapter 4.

39. The great student of medieval processionals, the books containing the texts, chants, and rubrics for processions, is Michel Huglo. He has catalogued the extant sources: see *Les Manuscrits du Processional,* Répertoire International des Sources Musicales, B 14, 1 (Munich, 1999), and 2 (Munich, 2004), and produced numerous studies on the subject, many of which are cited in the bibliography of those volumes. A short and useful introduction to the subject is found in his "The Cluniac Processional of Solesmes: Bibliothèque de l'Abbaye, Réserve 28," in *The Divine Office in the Latin Middle Ages,* ed. Margot E. Fassler and Rebecca A. Baltzer (Oxford, 2000), 205–12.

40. The opening procession into a church on a high feast day and its significance is discussed in my "Liturgy and Sacred History," and "The Meaning of Entrance." Gunilla Iversen has discussed these themes and the prophetic voice in *Chanter avec les anges. Poésie dans la messe médiévale: interprétations et commentaires* (Paris, 2001).

41. The miracles of Chartres were collected in the course of the twelfth century and first made available in Latin in the early thirteenth century, with Old French versions appearing in 1262 through the effort of Jean le Marchant. Pierre Kunstmann's edition contains a useful introduction and both the Latin and the Old French texts: *Miracles de Notre-Dame de Chartres* (Ottawa, 1974). That miraculous warnings of this sort were issued indicates a need to encourage attendance.

42. For the fairs of Chartres in the later Middle Ages, see Claudine Billot, *Chartres à la fin du Moyen Age* (Paris, 1980), 240–43.

43. Richard of St. Victor, *L'Edit d'Alexandre ou les trois processions,* ed. Jean Châtillon (Bruges, 1951), 2:38–39.

44. Raymond Brown, *The Birth of the Messiah* (New York, 1993), 450: ". . . let us explore the Samuel background in more detail. We remember that after the God-given conception and birth of her child, Hannah (or Anna—note the name) brought the child Samuel to the sanctuary at Shiloh and offered him to the service of the Lord (1 Sam 1:24–28). There she and her husband encountered the aged priest Eli, even as Mary and Joseph encountered the aged Simeon. We are told that Eli blessed Elkanah and Hannah (1 Sam 2:20), even as Simeon blessed Joseph and Mary (Luke 2:34). The Samuel story mentions women who were ministering at the door of the sanctuary (1 Sam 2:22), even as Luke describes Anna who 'never left the Temple courts; day and night she worshiped God, fasting and praying' (2:37)." For Brown's further commentary on this scene, see pp. 682–89.

45. Ibid., 450.

46. Egeria describes the feast (called in Jerusalem *Hypapante,* "The Meeting," with emphasis upon the preaching of the Gospel text, Luke 2:22–40): "Note that the Fortieth Day after Epiphany is observed here with special magnificence. On this day they assemble in the Anastasis. Everyone gathers, and things are done with the same solemnity as at the feast of Easter. All the presbyters preach first, then the

bishop, and they interpret the passage from the Gospel about Joseph and Mary taking the Lord to the Temple, and about Simeon and the prophetess Anna, daughter of Phanuel, seeing the Lord, and what they said to him, and about the sacrifice offered by his parents. When all the rest has been done in the proper way, they celebrate the sacrament and have their dismissal" (*Egeria's Travels to the Holy Land,* trans. John Wilkinson [Warminster, 1981], 128). The bibliography on the feast is vast: an introduction is provided in *Making History.*

47. See *The First Ordinary of the Royal Abbey of St.-Denis in France,* ed. Edward B. Foley (Fribourg, 1990), 486–87.

48. See *Paris, Bibliothèque Nationale, lat. 945,* fol. 96r for the texts of these prayers.

49. Here the texts are as found in *Chartres Bibliothèque Municipale 520,* fols. 340–341r. See the facsimile edition with introduction and notes by David Hiley, *Missale Carnotense Chartres Codex,* Monumenta Monodica Medii Aevi 6, 1 and 2 (Kassel, 1992). The original manuscript was destroyed in 1944.

50. The twelfth-century liturgical commentator Praepositinus of Cremona, for example, explains the meanings of the Greek word for the feast "Ypapanti." See his *Tractatus de Officiis,* ed. James A. Corbett (London, 1969), 1.81, "De ypapanti," pp. 56–57.

51. The special features of the ceremony at Chartres are detailed in the OC (see *L'Ordinaire chartrain du XIIIe siècle,* ed. Yves Delaporte [Chartres, 1953]), the OV (Ordo veridicus, see table 2 in the Appendix), the twelfth-century pontificals, and the thirteenth-century antiphoner, Rome, *Vatican lat. 4756.* (The Vatican Antiphoner is described in *Making History.*) The texts below are taken from the early thirteenth century Chartres Codex 520, *Missale Carnotense,* ed. David Hiley (Basil, 1992), folio 360.

52. Both the twelfth-century OV and the thirteenth-century OC contain the instruction to make a station "ante portam regiam." See OV, 13, and OC, 149.

53. OC, 149, and also in the OV.

54. PL 141:319–20. The sermon is believed to be authentic.

55. Sed praesentatio illa insignis et gloriosa fuit: movente enim Spiritu sancto, occurrerent ei sanctus propheta Simon et Anna sancta vidua et prophetissa, laudantes et benedicentes Dominum de Adventu Christi, sicut legitur in Evangelio, miracula praebentes. Christus namque in carne veniens, fratres, ostendebat pariter et humilitatis exemplum, et divinae pietatis indicia. Sicut in nativitate sua, cum jaceret humiliter in praesepio, nova stella, et laudibus angelicis celebrabatur in coelo: sic et modo cum parvulus infantulus praesentaretur in templo, ad declarandam divinitatem suam in carne latitantem corda prophetarum illuminabat Spiritus sanctus. Nos ergo qui illum verum Dominum et hominem adoramus, in memoriam Praesentationis ejus in templo celebramus hunc diem cum oblatione cereorum: per lumen cerei, divinitatem, per ceram significantes carnem ipsius virginalem. Apis enim et mellis, et cerae opifex sine coitu maris et feminae procreatur. Patet ergo quia Praesentatio Christi in templo processit ex obedientia legis, et nostra significativa oblatio est, ex dulci et venerabili memoria suae presentationis.

56. A new study of the rite in the medieval cathedral of Trondheim is forthcoming from David Chadd, "The Ritual of Palm Sunday: Nidaros in Context" (Turnhout, anticipated in 2006).

57. Delaporte commented at length on topography in OC, 45: "When one knows that at Rome the ceremonial of this day took place entirely in the Lateran and its immediate environs, one acknowledges that the procession of the palms such as we have described it, and such as took place in many of our churches, cannot have originated in imitation of a Roman ceremony. Rather it reproduces in a striking manner what was done in Jerusalem throughout antiquity, where, after gathering on the Mount of Olives, a cortege, entering the holy city, recalled the triumphal entrance of Christ. We observe that the topography of Chartres lends itself easily to this imitation: the hill of St. Cheron, east of the city, from which it is separated by the valley of the Eure, corresponds to the Mount of Olives, which rises east of Jerusalem, near the valley of the Cedron." Delaporte believed the topography of Paris was also adapted on Palm Sunday to reflect that of the city of Jerusalem for the procession and its ceremonies.

58. From Egeria's description of the festive practice, which was the model for those held throughout Europe (*Egeria's Travels,* 133): "At this the bishop and all the people rise from their places, and start off on foot down from the summit of the Mount of Olives. All the people go before him with psalms and antiphons, all the time repeating, 'Blessed is he that cometh in the name of the Lord.' The babies and the ones too young to walk are carried on their parents' shoulders. Everyone is carrying branches, either palm or olive, and they accompany the bishop in the very way the people did when once they went down with the Lord. They go on foot all down the Mount to the city, and all through the city to the Anastasis, but they have to go pretty gently on account of the older women and men among them who might get tired. So it is already late when they reach the Anastasis; but even though it is late they hold Lucernare when they get there, then have a prayer at the Cross, and the people are dismissed."

59. Ludwig Eisenhofer, *The Liturgy of the Roman Rite,* trans. A. J. and E. F. Peeler, ed. H. E. Winstone (Freiburg, 1961), 186–87, offers a succinct description of the Procession of the Palms in the medieval Roman rite: "From a principal church in the city the procession first of all made its way to another church usually situated outside the city walls. Then the procession returned to the city, solemnly recalling Christ's triumphal entry into Jerusalem. At the city gateway, or at the entrance of the principal church, the cross, or some other symbol of Christ, was publicly venerated in commemoration of the greeting which Christ received from the crowd that came out to meet him from the Holy City. It was here, too, that the *Gloria, laus* was sung, the triumphal hymn in honor of Christ the King, composed by Theodulf, Bishop of Orleans." In the later Middle Ages, statues of Christ were wheeled through some towns on various chariots, some of which were in the shape of a donkey.

60. The idea that all the community, including the relics of the saints, should be part of the procession is brought forth clearly in the eleventh-century *Liber tramitis,* prepared in Farfa and cited above (note 10). The procession is carefully ordered, with all the major relics, as well as with a highly prized statue of St. Peter (67–69). The inclusiveness created a sense of community extending far back in time, and promoted the sense that all stood together before the King in a powerful assembly on this feast day.

61. Wright, in "The Palm Sunday Procession," compares the action of the cathedral canons to that of the clergy of St. John in the Valley, and suggests ways in which the chanting and customs of individual churches conflicted.

62. The Ordinals of Chartres are discussed in Yves Delaporte's edition of Chartres 1058 (see note 51), and in my two papers, "The Disappearance of the Proper Tropes and the Rise of the Late Sequences: New Evidence from Chartres," *Cantus Planus 3,* ed. Laszlo Dobszay (Budapest, 1990), 319–35, and "Liturgy and Sacred History" (note 34). Craig Wright has used the ordinals and other sources for his detailed reconstruction in "The Palm Sunday Procession."

63. St. Ambrose, *Expositio evangelii secundum Lucam* 9.1–2, ed. M. Adriaen, CCSL 14 (Turnhout, 1957), 33.

64. This relic, the birthing chemise of the Virgin Mary, is the subject of several chapters of *Making History.* See also E. Jane Burns, "Saracen Silk and the Virgin's Chemise: Cultural Crossings in Cloth," *Speculum* 81 (2006): 365–97.

65. According to the twelfth-century OV, there were three kinds of greenery: flowering branches, palms which came from the cathedral clergy, and boxwood branches given out by the *prepositus* of St. Cheron. The olive and the palm branches were significant in medieval exegesis; the flowering branches were important for the depiction of the scene as found in the antiphon *Occurrunt,* discussed below.

66. See *Cartulaire de l'Abbaye de Saint-Père de Chartres,* ed. M. Guérard (Chartres, 1840), 1:21.

67. For the rubrics in *Chartres Bibliothèque Municipale 520,* see Hiley, facsimile of *Missale,* vol. 1, fols. 129r–130v; Wright, "The Palm Sunday Procession," has copied out the full rubrics from this source in an appendix, 358–59.

68. The bishops of Chartres in the eleventh and twelfth centuries were among the most powerful figures in Francia. Excommunication should be seen in the context of two important series of letters, those of Fulbert of Chartres and of Ivo of Chartres, both of whom used it as a skillful rod to rule their flocks and to inspire various modes of action from secular rulers. There was an elaborate ceremony at Chartres for the expulsion of the penitents from the church on Ash Wednesday (for which see OC, p. 97); discussion of this and similar ceremonies, and of the role that church ceremonies and rulings continued to play in the later Middle Ages, is found in Mary C. Mansfield, *The Humiliation of Sinners: Public Penance in Thirteenth-Century France* (Ithaca, 1995). A cemetery in Chartres for excommunicants

and for the unbaptized was outside the town walls by the river, near the Church of St. Andrew. Here, too, the topography of the town was used to make an important theological point.

69. PL 162:587.

70. Reginald Grégoire, *Homiliaires liturgiques médiévaux: Analyse de manuscripts,* Biblioteca studi medievali 12 (Spoleto, 1980). The ceremony of the palms in sixth- and seventh-century Rome may indeed have been closer to that described by Egeria in late fourth-century Jerusalem; this took place in the afternoon, as a preface to the reading of the Passion as found in the Gospel according to Matthew.

71. See, for example, Hiley, facsimile of *Missale,* vol. 1, fols. 131v–134v. The Communion chant text is of the bitter cup and recalls the agony in the garden.

72. For a study of the ritual surrounding the Ascension Day procession in Münster, with attention to changes in ordinals from the fifteenth through the nineteenth centuries, see Louis-Emil J. Lengeling, "Die Bittprozession des Domkapitels und der Pfarreien der Stadt Münster von dem fest Christi Himmelfahrt," in *Monasterium,* ed. Alois Schröer (Münster in Westfalen, 1966), 151–220. His study is attentive to ceremony and to the ways in which chant texts are important in shaping and defining the mode of action.

73. The ceremonial dragon has been much discussed by scholars but never situated in the context of the Ascension liturgy at Chartres. See especially, Yves Delaporte, "Une prétendue 'cérémonie bizarre' à la cathédrale de Chartres," in *La Voix de Notre Dame de Chartres* (1924), and Maurice Jusselin, "De quelques offices privilégiés auprès du chapître de Chartres, 1, Le Dragonnier de l'Église de Chartres," *Société archéologique d'Eure-et-Loir,* Mémoires, 17, p. 52. Reference to the beast in the accompanying chant text surely gave witness to its liturgical life presence at Chartres; for further discussion, see *Making History.*

74. For a sense of the range of this text, see the edition found in *Analecta hymnica,* vol. 7, p. 85 ff. and vol. 53, p. 111 ff. Both text and melody are discussed in Richard Crocker, *The Early Medieval Sequence* (Berkeley, 1977).

75. See OC, 128.

76. Rex omnipotens die hodierna
mundo triumphali redempto potentia
Victor ascendit caelos, unde descenderat.

Nam quadraginta, postquam surrexerat,
Diebus sacris confirmans pectora

Apostolorum, pacis cara relinquens oscula,
Quibus et dedit potestatem laxandi crimina,

Et misit eos in mundum baptizare cunctas animas
In patris et filii et sancti spiritus clementia;

Et converscens praecepit eis, ab Hierosolymis
Ne abirent, sed expectarent promissa munera.
Anon post multos enim dies mittam vobis spiritum paraclitum in terra,
Et eritis mihi testes in Hierusalem, Judea sive et Samaria.

Cum hoc dixisset, videntibus illis elevatus est nubes clara
Suscepit eum ab eorum oculis; intuentibus illis aera,

Ecce, stetere amicti duo viri in veste alba
Juxta dicentes: A quid admiramini caelorum alta?

Jesus enim hic, qui assumptus est a vobis ad patris dexteram,
Ut ascendit, ita veniet quaerens talenti commissi lucra.

O deus maris, poli, arvi, hominem, quem creasti, quem fraude subdola
Hostis expulit paradiso et captivatum secum traxit ad tartara.

Sanguine proprio quem redemisti deo
Judex cum veneris judicare saeculum
Illuc et provehis, unde prima corruit paradisi gaudia.
Da nobis petimus sempiternam requiem in sanctorum patria,
In qua tibi cantemus omnes Alleluia.

77. See *Chartres 138*, a twelfth-century lectionary that survives on microfilm.

78. Hebrews 10:19–20, "Having therefore, brethren, a confidence in the entering into the holies by the blood of Christ; A new and living way which he has dedicated for us through the veil, that is to say, his flesh, and a high priest over the house of God," is the text underlying this part of the sermon. Ivo finds in it a vivified road, one that allows the baptized to experience the triumph of acknowledging that sin and death, while still capable of winning battles, have ultimately lost the war.

79. This is the major theme of all his sermons, which include a short treatise on the sacraments of the Christian faith as foreshadowed by sacramental action of the Old Testament. See his "Sermo V sive Opusculum de convenientia veteris et novi sacrificii," in his *Sermones,* PL 162:535–62.

80. See Miri Rubin, *Corpus Christi: The Eucharist in Late Medieval Culture* (Cambridge, 1991).

81. See especially David Nirenburg, *Communities of Violence* (Princeton, 1996).

82. For discussion, see my *Gothic Song: Victorine Sequences and Twelfth-Century Reform in Paris* (Cambridge, 1993), which includes a section on the sequences of Chartres Cathedral. A second edition of this book is forthcoming from the University of Notre Dame Press, 2006.

83. For further discussion, see my "Liturgy and Sacred History."

84. The particulars of this interpretation, especially as related to the cult of the Virgin of Chartres, are in *Making History*.

85. See Jennifer Harris, "Thieves, Harlots, and Stinking Goats: Fashionable Dress and Aesthetic Attitudes in Romanesque Art," *Costume* 21 (1987): 4–15; and Janet G. Snyder, "From Content to Form: Court Clothing in Mid-Twelfth-Century Northern French Sculpture," in *Encountering Medieval Textiles and Dress: Objects, Texts, Images,* ed. Desirée G. Koslin and Janet E. Snyder (New York, 2002), 85–101,

86. For discussion of this theme, see my "Liturgy and Sacred History."

87. See *Making History,* chapter 11 for discussion of the chants used to process in and out of the portal throughout the year. For discussion of the chants sung at the Feast of the Holy Innocents and the allusions to the saints in the plays, see Susan Boynton, "Performative Exegesis in the Fleury *Interfectio Puerorum,*" *Viator* 29 (1998): 39–64. See also Kathleen Nolan, "'Ploratus et ululatus': The Mothers in the Massacre of the Innocents at Chartres Cathedral," *Studies in Iconography* 17 (1996): 9–141 and her "Ritual and Visual Experience in the Capital Frieze at Chartres," *Gazette des Beaux-Arts* 123 (1994): 53–72.

88. At Chartres, as in most places, readings from Revelation began after the octave of Easter and continued until Pentecost. The Book of Acts was also featured during this period. See OC, 126.

89. See "Liturgy and Sacred History" for a general discussion of portal sculpture as an embodiment of *adventus* themes. A classic reading of the West Portal is found in Adolf Katzenellenbogen, *The Sculptural Programs of Chartres Cathedral* (New York, 1959). For further bibliography on this and other aspects of Chartrain iconography, see Jan van der Meulen, Rüdiger Hoyer, and Deborah Cole, *Chartres: Sources and Literary Interpretation, A Critical Bibliography* (1989).

Seeing Is Believing

The Semiotics of Dynasty and Destiny in Muscovite Rus'

MICHAEL S. FLIER

> About the office of Christ, [the Muscovites] holde many fowle errours. . . . This hath brought them to an horrible excesse of idolatry, after the grossest & prophanest manner, giving unto their images al religious worship of prayer, thanksgiving, offerings, & adoration, with prostrating and knocking their heads to the ground before them, as to God himself. Which because they doo to the picture, not to the portraiture of the Saint, they say they worship not an idol, but the Saint in his image & to offend not God. . . . Their church walles are very full of them, richly hanged & set forth with pearle & stone. . . .[1]

In the sixteenth and seventeenth centuries, foreigners like Giles Fletcher seemed as appalled at the ubiquity of icons and their veneration in Muscovite Rus' as they were at the paucity of literate Muscovites at all levels of society.[2] The apparent complementarity between the orientation toward the pictorial and toward the written was not without reason. When the East Slavs accepted Christianity from the Byzantine Greeks in the late tenth century, the literacy that it fostered remained largely the province of the ecclesiastical elite. The inability to read predominated in Early Rus' and Muscovite Rus' (ninth through seventeenth centuries) and remained common in the Russian Empire well into the nineteenth century.[3]

From the first, the majority of the population of Early Rus' learned about the Old Testament kings and prophets, the Virgin Mary and Jesus Christ, and the creation of the Church from oral recitation in church services and from the depictions in murals and icons that occupied sanctified space. Considering that Church Slavonic and not the Russian vernacular was the language used in this setting, we can assume that oral communication about church teachings was less than optimal, obliging the faithful to rely even more heavily on visual representation. In Early Rus' and in Muscovite Rus', seeing and believing were closely intertwined.

The connection between visible and believable is a central motif in the grand narrative of the conversion itself.[4] The *Primary Chronicle,* our main source about the early history of Rus', records a series of episodes in which Grand Prince Volodimer is confronted directly or indirectly with visible evidence, marshaled to convince him to make the fateful choice of Christianity over Judaism and Islam, and specifically Greek Orthodox Christianity over the Roman Catholicism of the West. All the representatives from the competing monotheistic religions visit his court to proclaim the superiority of their faiths, but the Greek philosopher alone buttresses his position by showing Volodimer a cloth (*zapon"*) bearing a depiction of the Last Judgment to underscore the consequences of the wrong selection.[5] Later he hears the firsthand accounts of his emissaries, who have experienced the various services abroad. The description of their visit to Hagia Sophia in Constantinople creates an indelible image of the Byzantine rite for the grand prince:

> We did not know whether we were in heaven or on earth. Yet on earth there is no sight such as that, or such beauty, and we are unable to explain it. We know only that that is where God is totally present with men, and their service is better than any other country's, for any man who has tasted something sweet, does not accept bitterness afterwards.[6]

Pushed closer to the final decision, Volodimer demurs. After laying siege to the Greek city of Chersonesus in the Crimea and finally capturing it, he demands the hand in marriage of Anna, the sister of the Byzantine emperors Basil II and Constantine VIII. In response to the imperial call for his baptism prior to any marriage, Volodimer asks that Anna bring priests with her to Chersonesus to baptize him.[7] In his closest confrontation yet with the new faith, Volodimer is suddenly deprived of the visible world:

> . . . and at this time by God's design Volodimer was suffering from an eye disease and was unable to see anything and was quite distressed and could not decide what to do. And the princess [lit. empress] sent [a message] to him saying, "If you wish to rid yourself of this disease, then be baptized immediately; otherwise you will not be rid of this disease." Having heard this, Volodimer said, "If this is the truth, then truly the Christian God is great." And he gave orders for his baptism. And the bishop of Chersonesus along with the princess's priests instructed Volodimer, [and] baptized [him]. And as soon as he laid his hand on him, he regained his sight. And Volodimer saw this sudden healing and he praised God, saying, "Now I have perceived the true God." And when his retinue saw this, many were baptized.[8]

His vision miraculously restored, Volodimer is finally moved to accept Orthodox Christianity in 988/989 from the Byzantine Greeks. His progressive encounters with the painted image, the vision of his emissaries, and his own loss and recovery of sight help bring this latter-day Saul of Tarsus (Acts 9:1–22) to the realization that seeing and believing are fundamentally linked. In the Byzantine and now Rusian tradition, the visual image, sustained by word and ritual, appears the most efficacious way to convey the basic truths of Orthodox spirituality to the inhabitants of Rus' and their progeny. Such reliance on the image as a means to a greater truth beyond sensory perception—the basis for iconography itself—is a constant that connects the cultures of Early Rus' and Muscovite Rus'.

Inside an Orthodox church—for example, Kiev's Cathedral of the Holy Sophia or Moscow's Cathedral of the Dormition—the believer was surrounded by images of the sacred, from Christ Pantocrator and the Mother of God looking down from the highest reaches of the main cupola and apse to the individual saints who faced out directly toward the beholder at ground level. In the Byzantine *Kulturgut* transmitted to the East Slavs, the church was not simply a building set aside for prayer. It was intended to be a microcosm of the Kingdom of Heaven, a community of holy images, each with its place and function in the overall design, a community with which the true believer could interact. To enter an Orthodox church was to come into contact with an image of eternity, one in which elements and their spatial relationships all carried meaning within the larger whole.[9]

Predominately binary oppositions of high and low, front and back, left and right inform this world, establishing hierarchies that endure through their replication in each and every new church constructed. In this projection, the sacred eastern space in the sanctuary, representative of heaven, is reserved for officiating clergy, originally demarcated by a low barrier (eventually a high iconostasis) from the space for the congregation in the nave, representative of the terrestrial present. The final image a believer sees when exiting the nave is the Last Judgment painted on the inside western wall. In contrast to potential chaos and destruction in the world of time outside, the Orthodox church as a site of pictorial presentation and spatial division was a most powerful symbol of timeless harmony, order, beauty, and promise.

Semiotically the visible edifice and internal decoration of an Orthodox church may be understood as an icon of the Kingdom of Heaven, because, like all icons, it is a sign by virtue of its similarity to the object referred to — similarity in the form of its individual parts, in the relationships among them, or both. The iconic relationships are necessarily schematic, the visible representation of the sacred, the holy, the perfect limited by the resources of the material world. An icon of the Kingdom of Heaven, a holy person, or a sacred event from the past is by nature an imperfect distortion or shadow of the object represented, but it provides the tangible means by which the beholder can approach the holy while still locked into temporal existence on earth.[10]

Clifford Geertz has suggested that cultural patterns constitute "a model of" reality and "model for" reality.[11] From this perspective, such patterns are shaped by the meaning perceived in the object (model of) at the same time they bind that reality to themselves for the given community (model for). In this way, culturally determined signs from the past distinguish the significant from the insignificant in the present and provide a guide for seeing and interpreting reality in the future. It was especially through the visual that Rusian Orthodox culture came to shape the perception of reality through the development of specific cultural models that express value by means of cultural production. By examining visual artifacts of Muscovite culture, primarily those of its better documented elite culture, we gain a clearer understanding of how the center of that world was organized and how its leaders viewed their own place and the place of their people in the grand scheme of history and beyond.

The purpose of the present study is to exemplify the power and authority of visual culture in medieval Muscovy by tracing one thread of its evolution, the apocalyptic, from the mid-fourteenth century when Moscow began the "Gathering of the Russian Lands," until the late seventeenth century at the dawn of the Western-oriented Russian Empire of Peter the Great. I will argue that Orthodox theology interacting with the course of history provided Muscovy with a sense of its universal purpose, its mission, its destiny. The realization of that end implied in turn the continuity of the Muscovite branch of the ruling Riurikid dynasty.[12]

For elite culture at least, we find conviction that the convergence of Muscovy's historical moment and God's divine purpose was no mere coincidence. In addition to the bright colors and geometric angularity of Byzantine painted imagery, the principles of Orthodox iconography provided the tools for creating rituals that offered new means of affirming and reaffirming this conviction. To see Muscovite truth through the distinctive lens of Orthodox iconography was to believe in the salvific fate of a chosen people, whose historical narrative referred to Muscovy from the late fifteenth century on as the New Israel,[13] thereby justifying the introduction of concrete manifestations of the Holy Land into the visual landscape of central Moscow well into the sixteenth century. To call the city of Moscow the New Jerusalem was one thing; to build structures representing Golgotha or Jerusalem itself in the center of the city carried conviction to another level. Seeing was believing, until the demise of the dynasty in 1598 ushered in a period of turbulence, social upheaval, and foreign occupation, the so-called Time of Troubles.

Artifacts of the previously integrated culture were later susceptible to loss or reinterpretation, and it is here where we begin our story—at the end, so to speak—in 1678, when a church synod gathered in Moscow to consider, among other things, the origin and significance of a ritual performed in a number of ecclesiastical centers of Muscovite Rus' on Palm Sunday, the Sunday before Easter.

In Moscow, the head of the Russian Orthodox Church, the metropolitan (after 1589 the patriarch), enacted the role of Christ, seated on the back of a horse disguised as an ass. The tsar walked on foot, leading the ass by the reins in procession. In other centers of Rus', the chief ecclesiastical and secular officials, respectively, performed analogous roles. The synod, already facing the fact of the schism between the established church and the so-called Old Believers, was concerned about the ubiquity of the ritual, the effect of diminishing its importance in Moscow, especially since Nikon, the patriarch officially deposed a decade earlier, was very much alive and fiercely jealous of his former prerogatives. The investigation proved unsuccessful, as the report duly noted:

> And following the earlier, and quite thorough oral investigation of this matter, and a review of books, both ecclesiastical and annalistic, not even the slightest recollection of that ritual was found. . . . For this reason one can speculate that this ritual is not of ancient vintage, but was introduced into the Church shortly before our lifetime during the turbulent time [the Time of Troubles], when there was great unrest in this state, and it has been preserved continuously up until now.[14]

Seizing an opportunity when they saw one, the gathered clerics produced a proclamation that limited the ritual to the capital:

> That this ritual . . . for the glory of Christ our Lord and the reverence of [our] most devout crown-bearers ought to be performed only in the capital city of Moscow itself in the presence of the scepter-bearer by the patriarch himself and not by other prelates, even with the patriarchate vacant; for it is scarcely fitting that an act to which the patriarch alone is entitled, should be performed by a lower-ranking prelate. In yet other cities of the whole Great Russian State, let not a single prelate dare to have an ass prepared for procession on it to commemorate the Entry of our Lord into the city of Jerusalem, since neither is the tsar present nor does the rule book [tipikon] order it to be done, nor have we found a precedent for it in ancient piety.[15]

Apparently the special nature of the ritual had been denigrated by its spread. Equally clearly, the ruling elites of the 1670s had no idea where or when the ritual had been performed in the first place. But the focus of their contemporary interpretation was on the tsar ("for the glory of Christ . . . and the reverence of [our] most devout crown-bearers"); no one other than the patriarch himself was qualified to participate. And the reason for abandoning the ceremony outside of Moscow was not so much that a prelate could not participate. Rather, the absence of the tsar precluded the ceremony itself.

As the prime mover in the ritual, he was responsible for activating this living tableau of the Entry into Jerusalem. Crowned as God's representative on earth, he and he alone was entitled to perform the role of equerry before the living image of Christ. As the synod put it:

> . . . most of all, since our most pious autocrats deign to be in it, in order to show the Orthodox people the image of their humility and submission before Christ the Lord, for they have accepted a most humble custom, that when the patriarch has mounted the colt to commemorate the Lord's Entry into Jerusalem, they restrain their imperial haughtiness and hold fast to the reins of that ass's foal with their scepter-beautiful hands and thus lead it right to the cathedral church to serve Christ the Lord: this act is indeed praiseworthy, for many are moved by so much humility on the part of the Earthly Emperor before the Heavenly Emperor, and having grasped from God the spirit of grief inside themselves, they descend to soul-sparing humility and from the bottom of their hearts they cry out warmly to Christ the Lord, singing forth through reverent lips, "Hosanna in the highest, blessed is he who comes in the name of the Lord, King of Israel."[16]

The synod's decision declared the tsar to be the necessary pivotal participant to perform this particular topos of humility and Moscow to be its obligatory setting. It is the precise nature and location of that setting that helps to demonstrate the larger meaning of the Palm Sunday ritual and its significant complement, the Epiphany ritual, performed on January 6.

In their accounts of Muscovite Rus' in the sixteenth and seventeenth centuries, foreigners describe both ceremonies in some detail, locating them in the very heart of Moscow, within or near the fortress (Kremlin). Thus quite apart from their function of commemorating major feasts of the church, these two rituals, based on major processions involving the tsar himself, marked a political center in the sense that Clifford Geertz describes:

At the political center of any complexly organized society . . . there is both a governing elite and a set of symbolic forms expressing the fact that it is in truth governing. No matter how democratically the members of the elite are chosen (usually not very) or how deeply divided among themselves they may be (usually much more than outsiders imagine), they justify their existence and order their actions in terms of a collection of stories, ceremonies, insignia, formalities, and appurtenances that they have either inherited or, in more revolutionary situations, invented. It is these . . . that mark the center as center and give what goes on there its aura of being not merely important but in some odd fashion connected with the way the world is built. The gravity of high politics and the solemnity of high worship spring from liker impulses than might first appear. . . . In particular, royal progresses (of which, where it exists, coronation is but the first) locate the society's center and affirm its connection with transcendent things by stamping a territory with ritual signs of dominance.[17]

The spatial composition of the Moscow Kremlin had been determined primarily during the reign of Ivan III, the Great, in the last quarter of the fifteenth century. Because of Moscow's increasingly important role in Rus' as well as the Orthodox world as a whole, the inadequacies of the older provincial Moscow were obvious enough that a major rebuilding program was commenced inside the fortress in the 1470s, thus continuing the expansion begun a century before when Grand Prince Dmitri Donskoi enlarged the boundaries of the Kremlin to roughly their contemporary size and replaced the old wooden walls and earthen ramparts with limestone walls.[18]

Apparently built in the twelfth century as a western outpost for the thriving centers of Vladimir, Suzdal', and Rostov, Moscow in its prominent structures was inclined to emulate the northeastern style of royal architecture that favored the use of carved limestone for exteriors instead of the geometric masonry or stuccoed stone or brick-and-mortar types preferred elsewhere on East Slavic territory.[19] Limestone remained a favorite decorative material for window surrounds, portals, and cornices well into the seventeenth century.

In the most extreme cases, the surfaces of the twelfth- and thirteenth-century churches and palaces of the Suzdalian princes competed with the opulence of the icons and frescoes within, circumscribed by heavily carved corbel table friezes, interspersed with carved representations of saints and other figures, mythical beasts, and vegetal motifs, and articulated with engaged colonettes and recessed perspective arches over portals and gables.[20] These were monuments of architectural moment designed to be seen as much from without as within. Often situated on raised heights overlooking a nearby river, a royal ensemble of such buildings served as an imposing, somewhat theatrical, setting against which the power and authority of the ruling dynasty could be demonstrated.

Visually defining the royal and ecclesiastical center of a resurgent Moscow was surely at the core of the vast renovation projects undertaken and completed during the reigns of Ivan III (1462–1505) and Vasilii III (1505–33). Over the course of some fifty years, all the major structures surrounding the central Cathedral Square were erected or rebuilt, some by native Russians, but most by Italians, who brought more refined construction and engineering techniques to the task of creating a central space reminiscent of a grand Italian piazza, an outdoor stage suitable for solemn, large-scale pomp and circumstance.

The harmonious composition of the Cathedral of the Dormition (the site of the most important services, royal coronations, and the installations of metropolitans and patriarchs) demarcates the square on the north, across from the Cathedral of Archangel Michael (the royal necropolis) on the southeast side of the square and the Cathedral of the Annunciation (palace church) on the southwest. The churches dominated by bell towers at the eastern flank face the Faceted Hall (grand reception and banquet hall) at the northwest corner and the Golden Hall (throne room and vestibule) on the west. The fortress walls of the Kremlin were rebuilt and reinforced in heavy red brick of Italian design between 1485 and 1516. This central "stage" in the Kremlin was firmly in place by the time Ivan IV, the Terrible, was officially crowned tsar in 1547.

The earliest written documentation for the Epiphany and Palm Sunday royal rituals in Moscow is to be found in commentary from the English embassy led by Anthony Jenkinson in 1557–58, during the reign of Ivan IV.[21] What is especially interesting for our purposes is how much the purposely symbolic and abstract is intermingled with the more realistic and concrete.

For the Epiphany ritual, the Jenkinson report provides the following:

Every yeere upon the twelfe day [January 6] they use to blesse or sanc-
tifie the river Moska, which runneth through the citie of Moskovia,
after this manner. First, they make a square hole in the ice about 3. fath-
oms large every way, which is trimmed about the sides and edges with
white boords

Then about 9. of the clocke they come out of the church [Dor-
mition Cathedral] with procession towards the river. . . . [After the procession of men bearing tapers, crosses, and icons, and some 100 priests,
came] the Metropolitan who is led betweene two priests, and after the
Metropolitan came the Emperour with his crowne upon his head, and
after his majestie all his noble men orderly. Thus they followed the
procession unto the water, and when they came unto the hole that was
made, the priests set themselves in order round about it. And at one side
of the same poole there was a scaffold of boords made, upon which
stood a faire chaire in which the Metropolitan was set, but the Emper-
ours majestie stood upon the ice. After this the priests began to sing,
to blesse and to sense, and did their service, and so by that time that they
had done, the water was holy, which being sanctified, the Metropoli-
tane tooke a little thereof in his handes, and cast it on the Emperour,
likewise upon certaine of the Dukes, and then they returned againe to
the church with the priests that sate about the water: but y preasse that
there was about the water when the Emperour was gone was wonder-
ful to behold, for there came about 5000. pots to be filled of that water:
for that Muscovite which hath no part of that water, thinks himselfe
unhappy.[22]

During the actual Blessing of the Waters Ceremony on the ice, the emperor was described as standing bareheaded. The ceremony was called the
Procession to the Jordan' (*Khozhdenie na Iordan'*), the slightly altered, marked
form of Jordan with a palatalized *n'* to indicate that part of the Moscow
River exposed by the large hole in the ice.

Jenkinson continues his account with a description of the royal ceremony on Palm Sunday:

First, they have a tree of a good bignesse which is made fast upon two
sleds, as though it were growing there, and it is hanged with apples,

raisins, figs and dates and with many other fruits abundantly. In the midst of the same tree stand 5 boyes in white vestures, which sing in the tree before the procession. . . .

The float is followed in procession by young boys, priests, and half the Muscovite nobility. The centerpiece is the enactment of Christ's triumphant entry into Jerusalem on Palm Sunday:

> After them followed one halfe of the Emperours noble men: then commeth the Emperours majestie and the Metropolitaine, after this maner.
>
> First, there is a horse covered with white linen cloth down to the ground, his eares being made long with the same cloth like to an asses eares. Upon this horse the Metropolitaine sitteth sidelong like a woman: in his lappe lieth a faire book [the Gospels], with a crucifix of Goldsmiths worke upon the cover, which he holdeth fast with his left hand, and in his right hand he hath a crosse of gold, with which crosse he ceaseth not to blesse the people as he rideth.
>
> There are to the number of 30. men which spread abroad their garments before the horse, and as soone as the horse is past over any of them, they take them up againe and run before, and spred them againe, so that the horse doth always go on some of them. . . .
>
> One of the Emperours noble men leadeth the horse by the head, but the Emperour himselfe goyng on foote, leadeth the horse by the ende of the reine of his bridle with one of his hands, and in the other of his handes he had a braunch of a Palme tree: after this followed the rest of the Emperours Noble men and Gentlemen, with a great number of other people.[23]

The procession itself began at the Cathedral of the Dormition and made the rounds of the major Kremlin churches in Cathedral Square before returning to the Dormition for dismissal. Later accounts talk about the distribution of the branches of the tree by the metropolitan to the assembled throng, along with gifts to ranking members of the court.

A second version of the Palm Sunday ritual was introduced no earlier than 1561, when the procession moved beyond the walls of the Kremlin to the newly completed Jerusalem Chapel of the Church of the Intercession on the Moat in Red Square, now known as St. Basil's Cathedral. Following a brief service there, the procession made its way back to the Dormition inside the Kremlin walls. The third version, introduced by Patriarch Nikon in 1656, had a simple cross procession moving from the Dormition to the Jerusalem Chapel on Red Square. The tsar and patriarch participated in a service in the chapel, whereupon the float and the horse were brought around to a nearby raised daïs known as Golgotha (*Lobnoe mesto*), built in the mid-sixteenth century in emulation of the site of Christ's crucifixion in Jerusalem.[24] The patriarch and the tsar then performed their traditional roles, the former seated on the ass and the latter on foot, pulling the reins. With the float in the lead, the entire procession made its way through the Savior Gate into the Kremlin, returning finally to the Dormition for dismissal. Seventeenth-century engravings of the Epiphany ritual and Palm Sunday ritual reproduce many of the details described by eyewitnesses (see figures 1–4).

Figure 1 depicts the 1661 Epiphany ritual on the ice of the Moscow River from a vantage point south of the Kremlin. The wooden platform surrounding the hole in the ice is clearly visible in the foreground. In the detail shown in figure 2, one can make out the patriarch reading from the Gospel-book while priests cense the water of the Jordan'.

Figure 3 shows an engraving of the 1636 Palm Sunday ritual, with the procession leaving the Kremlin through the Savior Gate onto Red Square and snaking around from viewer right to left toward the Church of the Intercession at the upper left. The decorated tree leading the procession just approaches the church, followed by priests and various members of the nobility, including the boyars in tall fur hats. They in turn are followed by the tsar (flanked by his highest ranking boyars), who hold the reins of the "ass" on which the patriarch sits sidesaddle (see the detail in figure 4). The remaining nobility and other important Muscovites conclude the procession.

In earlier studies (see note 21), I proposed several levels of interpretation of the Epiphany and Palm Sunday rituals that clarify the ways in which these Muscovite royal progresses "locate the society's center and affirm its connection with transcendent things by stamping a territory with ritual signs of dominance." At the *performative level,* both rituals begin at the Cathedral of the Dormition, the site of the sacred Muscovite beginnings, the coronation and ordination of the tsar and metropolitan (patriarch), respectively. Following the litany on the day of Epiphany, the cross procession moves south

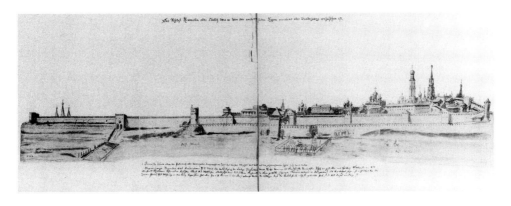

FIGURE 1. *The Epiphany Ritual in Moscow,* 6 January 1661. The platform surrounding the hole in the ice, the *Iordan'*, is in the foreground. Engraving from F. Adelung, *Al'bom Meierberga. Vidy i bytovye kartiny Rossii XVII veka* (St. Petersburg, 1903), Plate 74.

FIGURE 2. *The Epiphany Ritual in Moscow,* 6 January 1661. Detail of the *Iordan'*.

FIGURE 3. *The Palm Sunday Ritual in Moscow,* 10 April 1636. Engraving from French edition of Adam Olearius, *Vermehrte Newe Beschreibung der Muscowitischen und Persischen Reise* (Schleswig, 1656). Reproduced in Konstantin Nikol'skii, *O sluzhbakh russkoi tserkvi byvshikh v prezhnikh pechatnykh bogosluzhebnykh knigakh* (St. Petersburg, 1885), appendix.

from this locus through the gates of the Tainitsky Tower of the Kremlin wall out onto the frozen ice of the Moscow River, symbolizing the River Jordan. Following the Blessing of the Waters and the chief prelate's symbolic rebaptism of the tsar, himself, and by extension all of Muscovite Rus', the procession connects the space between the now sacred river and the sacred center inside the Kremlin walls.

On Palm Sunday, the procession in the first variant moves from the Dormition to the Cathedral of the Archangel Michael, the promise of current and future renewal made contiguous with the revered past of the dynastic necropolis. The procession moves on to the Cathedral of the Annunciation, thus linking the dynasty of the royal necropolis with the tsar's own palace church prior to the ceremonial return to the Dormition. In the second variant of the ritual, the procession establishes an enlarged zone of sym-

FIGURE 4. *The Palm Sunday Ritual in Moscow,* 10 April 1636. Detail of tsar and patriarch.

bolically charged space beyond the Kremlin walls to the east. The spiritual center of the Kremlin is linked to the newly constructed Church of the Intercession on the Moat, and most specifically to its chapel dedicated to the Entry into Jerusalem.[25] This connection of the Dormition inside the walls with a Jerusalem-based source outside the walls is analogous to that established in the Epiphany ritual described earlier. In both instances, the juxtaposition of Moscow and Jerusalem elevates the status of the Muscovite center. The identification of Moscow and Jerusalem is made even stronger in the third variant of the ritual, in which the Procession on the Ass occurs only after the service in the Jerusalem Chapel outside the Kremlin. Moscow is symbolically transformed into the very Jerusalem that Christ enters through the humble efforts of the tsar pulling the reins of the ass.

At the *historical level,* the Epiphany and Palm Sunday rituals are associated with the beginning and end of Christ's historical public ministry—his baptism by John the Forerunner in the River Jordan and his Entry into Jerusalem, which directly preceded his Passion, Crucifixion, and Resurrection. They also serve as typological prototypes of pivotal events in the Christian history of Rus'—the baptism of Grand Prince Volodimer in the Dnieper River and Ivan IV's triumphant return to Moscow following the great Orthodox Christian victory over the Muslim Tatars of Kazan' in 1552, an event that occasioned the building of the Intercession on the Moat as a votive church, many of whose chapels are dedicated to the feast days associated with Muscovite victories during the campaign.

Both rituals have resonance at the *eschatological level* as well, the Baptism of Christ as a mark of the end of mundane life and the beginning of a life reborn with a promise of eternity; the Entry as an index of the Second Coming of Christ, the General Resurrection, and the Last Judgment as foretold in the Book of Revelation and other apocalyptic literature. I have argued elsewhere that concern, especially among the elite, over the advent of the eighth millennium in 1492 had resulted in more than a century of textual and artistic references to the Apocalypse that coincided with Moscow's ascendance to leadership in the Orthodox world after the fall of Constantinople in 1453.[26] An apocalyptic mode resulted in an increasing interest in the thematics of the End Times and in the image of Moscow as the New Jerusalem and the Muscovites themselves as the New Israel. The regenerative power of the Blessing of the Waters for the entire people is evident in the extreme popular demand for the blessed water after the ceremony.

In the peculiarly Muscovite performance of the Procession on the Ass, Ernst Kantorowicz indicated how the very image of Christ on the ass was inspired by Roman imperial imagery, the representation of the emperor's triumphal departure (*profectio*) or arrival (*adventus*) into a city. Christ's Entry into Jerusalem could thus be viewed both as a historical event and as an eschatological one, the latter underscoring his role as messiah. In this case, the image of the Roman emperor led by a winged Victory is transformed into the King of the Jews led by an angel, associated with John the Forerunner, he who shall "prepare the way" (Mark 1:3). Kantorowicz cites the Muscovite tradition of the tsar leading the Procession on the Ass as a unique example in which the images of the historical and eschatological events are blended.[27]

It is with the *iconographical level* that we return to the theme established at the outset of this study, namely, the development and elaboration of visual or otherwise tangible means to generate, verify, and sustain belief. In my works mentioned previously, I have maintained that the Epiphany and Palm Sunday rituals were among the cultural artifacts used to affirm Muscovy's connection with transcendent things, namely, its salvific destiny as the last bastion of pure Christianity, whose ruler would stand before God at Golgotha in the role of the last emperor foreordained in the Revelation of Methodius of Patara. The inspiration for the visual presentation in both rituals was iconographic, to be sought in the iconic images of the Epiphany at Christ's Baptism and the Entry into Jerusalem.

In Orthodox iconography of the Epiphany (Theophany), Christ is always depicted as standing in the center of the River Jordan, humbling himself before John the Forerunner, who blesses his bare head while angels witness the event from the riverbank (fig. 5). In the Epiphany ritual in Moscow, the procession moved from the Kremlin out onto the ice of the Moscow River, not simply to the river's edge, but to the specially constructed *Iordan'* in the center of the frozen river, the framed hole in the ice where the actual Blessing of the Waters occurred. The first portion of the sanctified water was cast by the metropolitan on the tsar, standing bareheaded at the site. The fish and other animals depicted in the river found their counterparts in the horses and other animals that were brought to the *Iordan'* to drink after the procession had departed.

In analogous fashion, the iconography of the Entry into Jerusalem (fig. 6) accounts for visible clues present in the Palm Sunday ritual. The metropolitan in imitation of Christ sits sidesaddle on the "ass," in accordance with the depiction. The float with the boys singing in the tree finds its counterpart in the tree represented just outside the gates of Jerusalem as Christ approaches the city. These visual elements help to clarify and sustain for the beholder the connection between the ritual and the major feast being commemorated.

But the ritual representations of the ass and the tree differ from the corresponding depictions on the icon in interesting ways. On icons of the Entry, the ass is typically painted brown, grey, or more rarely, dark grayish-black.[28] Given the apparent availability of a horse, but not an authentic ass, for the ritual, the Muscovites could have simply added longer cloth ears to create

БГОѦВЛЕ НИЕ ГДНЕ

ІС. ХС.

FIGURE 5.   *Baptism of Christ (= Epiphany, Theophany).* Obverse of two-sided icon.
Novgorod, Cathedral of Holy Sophia, late fifteenth–early sixteenth century.

FIGURE 6. *Entry into Jerusalem.* Obverse of two-sided icon. Novgorod, Cathedral of Holy Sophia, late fifteenth–early sixteenth century.

the effect of an ass in imitation of the iconography, thus reproducing the color of the animal. They chose instead to clothe the animal (and its ears) in white linen down to the ground, creating a quite different effect with different interpretive ramifications.

Taking a cue from Kantorowicz' twofold interpretation of the Muscovite ceremony, I suggest that the image of Christ riding on an ass clothed in white linen has immediate apocalyptic connotations, recalling the impressive description from chapter 19 of Revelation, referring to God's reign, the marriage of the Lamb, and the vision of the mounted rider leading the armies of heaven into battle against the forces of evil:

> And a voice came out of the throne, saying, Praise our God, all ye his servants. . . . And I heard as it were the voice of a great multitude, and as the voice of many waters, and as the voice of mighty thunderings, saying Alleluia: for the Lord God omnipotent reigneth. Let us be glad and rejoice, and give honour to him: for the marriage of the Lamb is come, and his wife hath made herself ready. And to her was granted that she should be arrayed in fine linen, clean and white: for the fine linen is the righteousness of saints. . . . And I saw heaven opened, and behold a white horse: and he that sat upon him was called Faithful and True, and in righteousness he doth judge and make war. . . . And the armies which were in heaven followed him upon white horses, clothed in fine linen, white and clean. (Rev. 19:5–9, 11, 13)

The apocalyptic association of white linen and the rider-savior is reinforced by the commission around 1547 of an apocalyptic fresco cycle painted in the tsar's own Cathedral of the Annunciation. One prominent scene in the southwest transept shows the Righteous Judge, clothed in white linen, seated on a white horse leading the mounted heavenly host into battle, each warrior clothed in white linen (fig. 7).

The tree depicted in the Palm Sunday icon is typically a palm tree with boys cutting down branches to strew in the path of the approaching Christ. In the Moscow Palm Sunday ritual, the tree was constructed out of willow branches, palms being unavailable in such northern climes. The willow, an ancient harbinger of spring and the rebirth of nature, was a common substitute and served as the ubiquitous representation for Palm Sunday, so much

FIGURE 7.   *The Heavenly Host Follows the Righteous Judge into Battle* (Revelation 19:11–21). Fresco. Moscow, Cathedral of the Annunciation, southwest transept, mid-sixteenth century.

so that the holiday was also called *Verbnitsa* 'Willowtide' (from *verba* 'willow') and Willow Sunday.[29] The interesting detail that distinguishes the ritual tree from the iconographic depiction is the obligatory presence of fruit, and not just a single variety, but various sorts of fruit, some rather exotic, which could be associated with the Holy Land, e.g., apples, raisins, walnuts, carob pods, dates, figs, berries, cherries, lemons, oranges, and plums.[30] Although the symbolism of abundance and fertility is likely,[31] the sheer variety suggests a more concrete reference, especially since the tree is brought back to the Dormition, broken apart, and distributed to all those in attendance, highly prized gifts because of their healing properties. As the visiting Paul of Aleppo noted in 1655:

> The Russians have great faith in the aforementioned "tree" and take pieces of it with great reverence. We were told that it is beneficial for all ills, especially toothache; if a small piece of it is placed on a painful tooth, the pain goes away.[32]

In the setting of a Moscow self-identified as the New Jerusalem, the fruit-laden tree, like the horse clothed in white linen, has apocalyptic connotations. After the Last Judgment and the descent of New Jerusalem from heaven in the Book of Revelation, John provides a detailed description of the city's appearance, its twelve foundations and twelve gates, and then continues the narration:

> And the nations of them which are saved shall walk in the light of it: and the kings of the earth do bring their glory and honour into it. . . . And he shewed me a pure river of water of life, clear as crystal, proceeding out of the throne of God and of the Lamb. In the midst of the street of it, and on either side of the river, was there the tree of life, which bare twelve manner of fruits, and yielded her fruit every month: and the leaves of the tree were for the healing of the nations. (Rev. 21:24, 22:1−2)

The tree, so prominent in the ritual and visible to all those present, offered a tangible connection between the Moscow of history and the New Jerusalem of the Apocalypse, the promise of life eternal.

In annual royal ceremonies that each featured a procession going beyond the high walls of the Muscovite center, the heads of church and state had effectively stamped out new territory of transcendent import. The tsar and the metropolitan brought living icons of renewal and rebirth into direct contact with ritual objects associated with Jerusalem, each image containing elements that spoke not only to the historic past but to an apocalyptic future that signaled a remarkable destiny for this latter-day Chosen People. Passing out through the gates of the Muscovite fortress, as if through the royal doors of a massive iconostasis, the ceremonies had the effect of a macro-liturgy with the city as sanctuary and the space beyond as nave, a service in which both the blessed water and the Tree of Life were appropriate gifts for a cosmic mass, distributed at the end to the faithful who have entered into the New Jerusalem, thus fulfilling the promise of Revelation 22:13:

> I am the Alpha and the Omega, the beginning and the end, the first and the last. Blessed are they that do his commandments, that they may have right to the tree of life, and may enter in through the gates into the city.

But as the reaction of the synod in 1678 so clearly demonstrates, this particular vision of the Muscovite tsar and the salvation of Rus' was compromised by the demise of the Riurikid dynasty, the ensuing Time of Troubles, and the turmoil of reform and schism in the mid-seventeenth century. Questions of imminent apocalypse ceased to be the monopoly of the Muscovite center, the royal court, and the official church.[33]

As a consequence of this shift, the predominately positive and hopeful images of the Apocalypse presented in public display by the ruling elite—the rider on the white horse, the holy water, the tree of life—were counterbalanced by the terror of the Apocalypse in the form of images especially popular among the Old Believers in illustrated manuscripts and icons—Satan in various guises, the seven-headed crimson beast with ten horns, the Whore of Babylon, Armageddon, and the like. With these very distinct views of the Russian tsar's role in the End Times—perceived now as savior, now as Antichrist—the respective practitioners of high official culture and low popular culture competed visually and verbally for the hearts and minds of the Muscovite faithful throughout the seventeenth century.

NOTES

1. Giles Fletcher, *Of the Russe Commonwealth* (1588–89, pub. 1591), facsimile edition with variants, introduction by Richard Pipes, glossary-index by John V. A. Fine, Jr. (Cambridge: Harvard University Press, 1966), fol. 97v.

2. Ibid., fols. 85–86. Cf., for example, Richard Chancellor (1553, pub. 1589), *Rude & Barbarous Kingdom: Russia in the Accounts of Sixteenth-Century English Voyagers,* ed. Lloyd E. Berry and Robert O. Crummey (Madison: University of Wisconsin Press, 1968), 35–36; and Adam Olearius (1634, 1636, 1639, 1643, pub. 1647, 1656), *The Travels of Olearius in Seventeenth-Century Russia,* trans. and ed. Samuel H. Baron (Stanford, CA: Stanford University Press, 1967), 252–58.

3. The census of 1897 placed literacy at 21 percent of the general population of the Russian Empire. The rate ranged according to locale and gender, from a low of around 6 percent in rural areas to over 70 percent among the male population of Moscow Province; see Jeffrey Brooks, *When Russia Learned to Read: Literacy and Popular Literature, 1861–1917* (Princeton, NJ: Princeton University Press, 1985), 4. See also Daniel Rowland, "Biblical Military Imagery in the Political Culture of Early Modern Russia: The Blessed Host of the Heavenly Tsar," *Medieval Russian Culture,* vol. 2, ed. Michael S. Flier and Daniel Rowland, California Slavic Studies 19 (Berkeley: University of California Press, 1994), 185.

4. For a judicious review of the historical circumstances surrounding the conversion, see Simon Franklin and Jonathan Shepard, *The Emergence of Rus, 750–1200* (New York: Longman, 1996), 139–80.

5. *Polnoe sobranie russkikh letopisei (PSRL),* vol. 1, 2nd ed. (Leningrad, 1926), cols. 84.18–106.14.

6. Ibid., col. 108.18–25.

7. Ibid., cols. 109.1–111.4.

8. Ibid., col. 111.4–18.

9. Eusebius, *History of the Church,* ch. 10, pt. 4; Maximus the Confessor, *The Mystagogy of the Church,* chs. 1–3; St. Germanus, *On the Divine Liturgy,* trans. Paul Meyendorff (Crestwood, NY, 1984), 42–43; Arkhiepiskop Veniamin, *Novyi Skrizhal' ili ob"iasnenie o tserkvi, o liturgii i o vsekh sluzhbakh i utvariakh tserkovnykh* (St. Petersburg, 1899), chs. 1–2; Otto Demus, *Byzantine Mosaic Decoration: Aspects of Monumental Art in Byzantium* (Boston, 1955), ch. 1.

10. Cf. the second apologia of John of Damascus: "For we yearn to see how [God] looked, as the apostle says,'Now we see through a glass darkly.' Now the icon is also a dark glass, fashioned according to the limitations of our physical nature" (cited from John of Damascus, *On the Divine Images: Three Apologies against Those Who Attack the Divine Images,* trans. David Anderson [Crestwood, NY, 1980], 53).

11. Clifford Geertz, "Religion as a Cultural System," in *The Interpretation of Cultures* (New York: Basic Books, 1973), 93. First published in *Anthropological Approaches to the Study of Religion,* ed. M. Banton (London: Tavistock, 1966).

12. According to the *Primary Chronicle,* the beginnings of rulership in Rus' were traced to the legendary Riurik (died 879), who was invited together with his two Viking brothers to bring order to the northern East Slavs. The Muscovite line of the Riurikid dynasty lasted until the death of the childless Fedor, son of Ivan IV, in 1598.

13. Daniel E. Rowland, "Moscow—The Third Rome or the New Israel?" *Russian Review* 55 (1996): 595 ff.

14. *Akty sobrannye v bibliotekakh i arkhivakh Rossiiskoi imperii,* vol. 4: *1645–1700* (St. Petersburg, 1836), no. 223, p. 308.

15. Ibid., p. 309.

16. Ibid., pp. 308–9.

17. Clifford Geertz, "Centers, Kings, and Charisma: Reflections on the Symbolics of Power," in *Local Knowledge: Further Essays in Interpretive Anthropology* (New York: Basic Books, 1983), 124. First published in *Culture and Its Creators,* ed. Joseph Ben-David and T. N. Clark (Chicago: University of Chicago Press, 1977).

18. *PSRL,* vol. 25 (Leningrad, 1949), 394.

19. This is by no means to deny the very real influences from other parts of Rus' on Muscovite architecture, especially from Novgorod and Pskov. The incorporation of northwestern features was a demonstration of Moscow's synthetic self-perception.

20. See N. N. Voronin, *Zodchestvo Severo-vostochnoi Rusi,* 2 vols. (Moscow, 1961–62), and William Craft Brumfield, *A History of Russian Architecture* (Cambridge: Cambridge University Press, 1993), 43–63, 83–106.

21. For detailed accounts of foreign and domestic documentation of the rituals and their interpretation, see Michael S. Flier, "The Iconology of Royal Ritual in Sixteenth-Century Muscovy," in *Byzantine Studies: Essays on the Slavic World and the Eleventh Century,* ed. Speros Vryonis, Jr. (New York, 1992), 53–76; idem, "Breaking the Code: The Image of the Tsar in the Muscovite Palm Sunday Ritual," in *Medieval Russian Culture,* vol. 2, ed. Michael S. Flier and Daniel Rowland (Berkeley: University of California Press, 1994), 213–42; idem, "Court Ceremony in an Age of Reform: Patriarch Nikon and the Palm Sunday Ritual," in *Religion and Culture in Early Modern Russia and Ukraine,* ed. Samuel H. Baron and Nancy Shields Kollmann (DeKalb: Northern Illinois University Press, 1997), 73–95.

22. Anthony Jenkinson's testimony in Richard Hakluyt, *The Principall Navigations Voiages and Discoveries of the English Nation,* facsimile edition, introduction by David Beers Quinn and Raleigh Ashlin Skelton (Cambridge, 1965), 341. First published in London in 1589.

23. Ibid., 341–42.

24. Details on the construction of *Lobnoe mesto* are sketchy. It is supposedly mentioned in 1547 when Ivan IV appealed for support from the crowds gathered in Red Square. It was the tribune from which royal declarations were read to the people, including announcements of the birth of an heir to the throne, the death of the tsar, and the naming of his successor. See Nikolai Karamzin, *Istoriia gosudarstva Rossiiskogo* (St. Petersburg, 1842), bk. 2, vol. 8, col. 64 and n. 182. The Karamzin citation is based on the Archival *Stepennaia kniga* of Khrushchev, but there is no such entry in the published *Stepennaia kniga, PSRL* 21, pts. 1–2 (St. Petersburg, 1908–13). It was rendered in masonry in 1598/99; see *PSRL* 34 (Moscow, 1978), 202, and B. A. Uspenskii, *Tsar' i patriarkh: Kharizma vlasti v Rossii (Vizantiiskaia model' i ee russkoe pereosmyslenie)* (Moscow: Iazyki russkoi kul'tury, 1998), 455 n. 52.

25. For an analysis of the layout and naming of the eight chapels arrayed around the tower church devoted to the Intercession, see Michael S. Flier, "Filling in the Blanks: The Church of the Intercession and the Architectonics of Medieval Muscovite Ritual," in *Kamen' kraegg"l'n": Rhetoric of the Medieval Slavic World,* ed. Nancy S. Kollmann et al. (= *Harvard Ukrainian Studies* 19, nos. 1–4, 1995), 120–37.

26. Michael S. Flier, "Till the End of Time: The Apocalypse in Russian Historical Experience before 1500," in *Orthodoxy in Russian Historical Experience,* ed. Valerie Kivelson (University Park: Pennsylvania State University Press, 2003), 127–58.

27. Ernst H. Kantorowicz, "The 'King's Advent' and the Enigmatic Panels in the Doors of Santa Sabina," *Art Bulletin* 26, no. 4 (1944): 229.

28. I have found a few examples of the ass painted white, but none earlier than mid-late sixteenth century from Muscovy. See, for example, Tamara Talbot Rice, *Icons* (London, 1990), plate 51 (mid-late sixteenth century), and Konrad Onasch and

Annemarie Schneider, *Icons: The Fascination and the Reality* (New York, 1997), 103 (seventeenth century).

29. See Michael S. Flier, "Sunday in Medieval Russian Culture: *Nede'lja* versus *Voskresenie*," in *Medieval Russian Culture*, vol. 1, ed. Henrik Birnbaum and Michael S. Flier, vol. 1 (Berkeley: University of California Press, 1984), 105–49. *Verbnitsa* 'willow-tide' is itself no doubt a relic of the earlier pagan celebration of the rites of spring.

30. The inventory varies, depending on the source of information, but all the varieties of fruit listed here are mentioned in foreign accounts and in Muscovite ceremonials.

31. Robert O. Crummey, "Court Spectacles in Seventeenth-Century Russia: Illusion and Reality," in *Essays in Honor of A. A. Zimin* (Bloomington: Indiana University Press, 1995), 133.

32. *Puteshestvie antiokhiiskogo patriarkha Makariia v Rossiiu v polovine XVII veka, opisannoe ego synom, arkhidiakonom Pavlom Aleppskim,* pt. 3 (Moscow, 1898), 179.

33. See Robert O. Crummey, *The Old Believers and the World of Antichrist: The Vyg Community and the Russian State, 1694–1855* (Madison: University of Wisconsin Press, 1970), 14 ff; idem, "Religious Radicalism in Seventeenth-Century Russia: Re-examining the Kapiton Movement," *Forschungen zur osteuropäischen Geschichte* 46 (1992): 178 ff.

The King's Advent Transformed

The Consecration of the City in the Sixteenth-Century Civic Triumph

GORDON KIPLING

I

If I were to choose but one image that might best exemplify the ritual, liturgical, and theatrical motives of the late-medieval royal entry, it would be this image of the Spanish Merchants' Pageant for the entry of the future emperor Charles V into Bruges in 1515 (fig. 1). As Prince Charles makes his way through the city, this image invites him to see his entry into Bruges as a type of Christ's entry into Jerusalem. An actor kneels before the gates of a city. In one sense, its gates and towers look very earthly, for they resemble the cityscape of Bruges itself.[1] In another sense, however, the city depicted in this image seems celestial, for it is set within the arch of the sun and moon and populated, in part at least, by angels. One could be forgiven for mistaking it for the celestial Jerusalem that will descend from God at the end of time to locate the center of New Heaven and New Earth. And in yet another sense, the cityscape seems to refer particularly to the literal Jerusalem, the capital city of an earthly kingdom that longs for its redemption at the hand of a crusader king. The middle angel thus offers Charles a blazon of arms of the medieval Kingdom of Jerusalem, while "declaiming in a high voice that

FIGURE I. Spanish Merchants' Pageant, Bruges, 1515. Angels present the Crown of Jerusalem to Charles, Archduke of Austria. Vienna, Österreichische Nationalbibliothek, MS 2591, 41ʳ. By permission of A. N. L. picture archives, Vienna.

which was once said to Gideon: 'The Lord is with thee, O most valiant of men! Go in this thy strength, and thou shalt deliver Jerusalem.'" The image, in fact, represents all three: at the advent of its Christ-like lord, Bruges becomes a holy city in the image of the celestial Jerusalem, and the presence of its Lord redeems the earthly city just as, it is hoped, Charles as a crusader king will one day deliver the earthly Kingdom of Jerusalem from its bondage. The advent of the king, as represented in the pageant imagery, thus has the power to transform the earthly city into a type of the holy city of Jerusalem.[2]

As "metaphysical theatre,"[3] this pageant design marshals its potent symbolism to stage an epiphany for Prince Charles. One way it does this is by means of the three angels' offering of gifts to the actor who portrays Prince Charles. Although not Magi, the three of them bear gifts. I do not mean to suggest that the actors intend a direct allusion to the Magi, only that their offerings fulfill the same revelatory function as did the gifts of the Magi. By offering these three symbolic gifts — blazon, crown, and keys — to the prince, they perform a symbolic act of recognition and acclamation. Although delivered by the angels, they come from God as a sign of divine favor. They mark the prince out from all others as the Elect of the Lord. Further, because they are highly charged symbolic gifts, they make manifest the spiritual idea of Christian kingship that Charles represents. This act of gift-giving — this epiphany — stresses that Charles derives his right to rule not primarily from his earthly inheritance, but rather from an act of divine election. The crown and keys which represent his right to rule the people of Bruges come to him as a gift directly from God. Consider again that blazon of arms. The "cross potent" of the kings of Jerusalem displays not his familial lineage, but his spiritual one. The middle angel presents that gift to him along with the divine blessing once bestowed upon Gideon, whom the pageant artist imagines to have been a former savior of Jerusalem. As this gift makes clear, Charles rules the holy city — whether Jerusalem or Bruges — because he is Gideon's spiritual heir, not because he is Archduke Philip's earthly son. Just as Charles derives his kingly privileges as gifts from God, so he must now exercise those privileges in the image of God's rule by governing the people of Bruges as if they were citizens of the holy city. To make its point, the pageant design requires the presence of Prince Charles. The pageant is the symbol, but he is the referent. As "metaphysical theatre," it makes Prince Charles' identity as the Anointed One visible to mortal eyes.

Thanks to the remarkable, illustrated festival book—the first of its kind in Europe—published by Remi du Puys to commemorate this entry, the Bruges entry of 1515 became one of the touchstones of the form, and we find later royal entries throughout northern Europe pillaging its illustrations for inspiration.[4] For our purposes, however, this Bruges image serves merely as a monument to the past, not as a signpost to the future. It may well orient us to where we have been and allow us to measure the length of our journey once we have come to the end of it, but it will not help much in planning our route.

During the sixteenth century, the idea of the king's advent both endures and transforms itself into quite a different act of metaphysical theater from the one embodied in the Spanish Merchants' Pageant for Prince Charles in 1515. Particularly in the Low Countries, the medieval theatrical ritual of royal inauguration and popular affirmation transforms itself by stages into quite a different ritual. In the first stage of this transformation, the royal entry increasingly hedges about its staged kingly epiphanies with qualifications and limitations; in the second stage, it then dramatizes the power of the city, rather than that of God, to both make and unmake kings. These stages, I think, are succinctly illustrated in two famous entries that took place in the town of Antwerp: the joint entry of Emperor Charles V and his son Philip of Spain (1549) and the entry of Francis of Anjou (1582). The Antwerp entry of 1549, for instance, which has been called the "greatest Imperial fête of the [sixteenth] century,"[5] formed the climactic act of Charles V's campaign to join the Low Countries to Spain, to establish his son, Prince Philip, as his undoubted heir throughout the Habsburg dominions, and perhaps even to ensure Philip's election as Holy Roman Emperor.[6] Similarly, Anjou entered Antwerp in 1582 as part of a scarcely less portentous campaign to wrest the sovereignty of the Netherlands from Philip II. Both entries attempted to use the metaphysical theater of the royal entry in calculated acts of monarchal transformation, although to strikingly different effects. Because of the political importance of these two entries, and also because illustrated accounts of them were published in several languages and distributed all over Europe, they became, perhaps, the two most influential royal entries of the century.

II

Consider the apotheosis which the citizens arranged for Prince Philip to experience at the climactic last pageant of the Antwerp entry of 1549 (fig. 2) as the procession neared the Abbey of St. Michael.[7] If we glance from this Antwerp pageant image, in which Prince Philip enjoys an apotheosis and heavenly coronation, to the Bruges pageant image of 1515, in which Charles is receiving the keys, blazon, and crown of Jerusalem, we can see that both speak in approximately the same symbolic vocabulary. Both represent the prince's entry into the city as a spiritual metaphor: his arrival is an earthly model of the divine *figura* or type of the Christian apotheosis and entry into heaven. So, too, the bestowals of heavenly crowns in both cases figure the earthly accession to sovereign power and proclaim that both result from divine election. They both stage a moment of epiphany in which the prince is revealed to those watching as a *christus,* the Lord's Anointed One. The only acceptable response to such an epiphany on the part of those watching is acclamation: Blessed is he who comes in the name of the Lord. From this point of view, Philip's celestial coronation (fig. 2) is only a more extravagant, imperial, version of the more modest image of Charles' apotheosis (fig. 1).

Despite these similarities, it is hard to escape the impression that Philip's coronation is somehow overstated, that it is hedged about with limitations and qualifications not present in Charles' apotheosis.[8] The legend emblazoned across the upper frieze just above Philip's celestial coronation, for instance, necessarily provides the verbal context within which we must interpret this image: "Non est poestas nisi a deo" (There is no power except from God). Is this quotation from Paul's epistle to the Romans (13:1) meant to support this epiphany by insisting that Philip's power derives from God, or is it meant to qualify this scene, by insisting that true power derives from God and not a mere man such as Philip? Or consider how the presence of God the Father in this image further qualifies and diminishes Philip. The Bruges pageant of 1515 had sensibly left the Almighty out of its scene of divine election. By having mere angels deliver the crown, blazon, and keys as tokens of divine election, the image positions Charles as the most important figure in the scene. By including God the Father, the imperial pageant of 1549 instead divides the focus between the image of the Almighty and that of the kneeling Philip. But such a division in focus cannot help but

FIGURE 2. Final Antwerp Pageant at the Abbey of St. Michael, 1549. Apotheosis of Prince Philip. Grapheus, *La tresadmirable . . . entree,* N3ᵛ. By permission of the Folger Shakespeare Library.

disadvantage Philip. The pageant deviser thus not only includes God the Father in the scene, he also brings in the Almighty's entire celestial court as an illustration of the immense status of the Father. To begin with, the Father is attended by a series of angelic women named Majesty, Virtue, Glory, Power, Fame, and Immortality. Then there is the entire, marvelous machine of heaven composed of bright angels and blazing lamps, the whole stellar machine turning about a central sunburst just behind the Father's head so as to define it as a creation of the Divine Mind. These serve as allegorical and stellar epiphanies of the Father's nature, not Philip's. All these paraphernalia of the divine court establish the Almighty—quite properly—as a far more dominant figure than Philip. After we view that image, we can only read its legend in one way: God is the one with all the power. Because mere men like Philip only receive derivative power during the Father's pleasure, they necessarily kneel in submission before the Almighty.

One may wish to object, of course, that Philip represents the Son, that the Son's nature is theologically indivisible from that of the Father, so that the court of heaven belongs as much to the Son as to the Father. But in fact, the image does not seem to go very far down that road. Rather, it seems much more intent on distinguishing heavenly from worldly power and emphasizing the derivative nature of worldly glory. The Bruges pageant of 1515 would surely also accept such a division between worldly and heavenly glory, but, as we have seen, it prefers to keep the Almighty off stage and thus refuses to allow the Lord's presence to compete with Prince Charles' own glory. The Antwerp pageant of 1549 is all the more remarkable, then, not only because it permits such a competition, but it actually makes that competition its primary subject matter.

The divided focus of this image, I would suggest, reveals a considerable confusion about the purpose of the entry as a whole, even though the people of Antwerp were doing their best to provide not just an impressive acclamation of the Habsburg state, but indeed an extraordinarily magnificent and loyal one.[9] For the citizens of Antwerp, however, royal entries like this were almost exclusively staged on the occasion of the Duke of Brabant's *blijde inkomst* or *joyeuse entrée,* a ceremony that marked his accession.[10] These shows are about the making of sovereigns; they characteristically serve to mark the inauguration of the city's sovereign lord. The ceremony thus typically begins just outside the city walls where the would–be duke must deliver a "serment" in which he proclaims a grant of rights and privileges for the people. In return, he receives the homage of Antwerp's chief nobles and representative citizens and is formally invested with his new identity as the sovereign Duke of Brabant. Only at the end of this ritual transformation might the duke then make his first advent as Antwerp's sovereign lord. He symbolically performs his role by entering the city for the first time, and the implications of his first, sovereign manifestation might be symbolically explored in pageants that punctuated the route of his procession.

But if the citizens of Antwerp regarded the *joyeuse entrée* as an essential part of their duke's inauguration ritual, then what was the purpose of the 1549 triumph? No sovereign was inaugurated, and no significant ritual transformation took place. Philip, it is true, was being formally invested as "Marquis of the Holy Roman Empire" on this occasion, but that dignity was more a title of honor than an office, and it carried few, if any, constitutional implications.[11] At best, the ceremony merely formalized the status he already enjoyed as deputy to his father, who remained Antwerp's unquestioned sovereign.[12] The presence of his father, the emperor, in the procession could thus only emphasize Philip's subordinate position as a marquis. At the heart of this, the "greatest Imperial fête of the century," there thus lay a grave conceptual and ritual awkwardness. The entry was primarily occasioned by Philip's arrival, and it was undeniably meant to enhance his reputation, not that of his father. But by receiving an heir apparent in a way usually reserved for the inauguration of new dukes, and with an extravagance of spectacle never before attempted, might not Antwerp seem too eager in anticipating the reign of a future sovereign lord and hence the demise of their present duke? Perhaps to dispel such a thought, the pageants often strive to award their primary praise to Charles while suggesting that Philip's virtues are mere reflections of his father's.

The presence of Philip's father was probably intended to strengthen Philip's credentials by lending the authority of a popular sovereign to this ritual, but instead it creates an extremely problematic division of focus. Consider, for example, the divided focus which results even from an attempt to create an image of common purpose. At the entrance to Antwerp's market square, images of the emperor and his son, depicted as Hercules and Atlas respectively, stand atop a triumphal arch (fig. 3) between two double-headed Habsburg eagles, to form an emblem of universal empire (G, L3ᵛ–L4ᵛ;

De hooch
te.l.voetē.
De brepte
rruiij.voe.
De diepte
rr.voeten.

FIGURE 3.   Antwerp Pageant Arch at entrance to Market Square, 1549. Emperor
Charles V and Prince Philip represented as Hercules and Atlas. Grapheus, *La tresadmirable . . . entree,* MI[r]. By permission of the Folger Shakespeare Library.

C, 2:177–80). Like Atlas and Hercules, according to the inscription on the arch, Emperor Charles V (with his imperial crown) and his son, Prince Philip, effortlessly bear the globe of the world upon their shoulders.[13] Now, this image clearly means to pay equal tribute to both Charles and Philip: both lend an equal shoulder to bear up the world, both gesture identically with their swords, both strike virtually the same pose. Such a display of equality, however, tends to confuse further the inaugural purposes of this spectacle. Which is the king who is making this advent to his people? Are they both coming to their people? If so, what is the meaning of this double advent? What, exactly, are the people of Antwerp being asked to acclaim? More importantly, doesn't such a display of equality as this tend to emphasize differences? Charles V, for instance, wears a closed crown of imperial rule, while Philip wears a merely royal one. On the one hand, Charles, the imperial father, enters the city full of experience, political accomplishment, and popularity. Symbolically speaking, he had been successfully bearing the globe of the world upon his imperial shoulders for quite some time. On the other hand, Philip, the royal son, enters Antwerp—indeed the Netherlands—for the first time. His relative youth and inexperience beside his father mean that the citizens must view him in terms of his future potential rather than his past accomplishments. Philip cannot in fact appear as the equal of Charles. As son to father, as vassal to lord, as inexperienced youth to reverend age, he must necessarily defer in status and accomplishment to his greater parent. Perhaps he will one day bear the world upon his shoulders as his father has done. Perhaps, indeed, we may wish to view this image as embodying the emperor's wish to transfer the imperial burden to his son's shoulders. If so, however, this image more clearly defines a future objective of Charles V's imperial will than it does the inaugural purpose of Philip's entry into Antwerp. On the present occasion, at least, Philip will necessarily appear here as only the helpmeet of Charles, a pious son attempting to shoulder part of his father's burden.

From the viewpoint of metaphysical theater, this division of focus is disastrous for Philip. Royal entries, after all, were essentially designed for inaugural purposes. Because they celebrate the first advent of the new king, they necessarily focus sharply upon a single ruler. He must enter the city as the long-expected Savior making his First Advent to his people, his first manifestation as their king. By contrast, this Antwerp entry finds itself acclaiming Philip's coming as the advent of one who is certainly *not yet* the city's lord, and it does so in the very presence of an emperor—Charles—whom the city long ago recognized as its rightful lord. Further, even as these pageants receive Philip respectfully, they continue to reaffirm their loyalty to Charles as their one, true lord. The show's division of focus can thus only be resolved by representing Philip as secondary to his father. As a consequence, many of the pageants often represent the meaning of Philip's advent as hedged about with qualifications, some intentional, others perhaps not.[14]

Another of Antwerp's triumphal arches (fig. 4) attempts to modify the inaugural purposes of the royal entry by representing Philip's present entry into Antwerp merely as a hopeful sign of a future imperial advent (G, I4^r–K1^v; C, 2:166–68). If he could not yet be received as the Anointed One, then perhaps this entry might at least be treated as a portent of his future advent. At an arch erected in Koepoortstraat, Philip thus stands between Ascanius, son of Aeneas, and Servius Tullius, who is to succeed Tarquinius Priscus as king of Rome. The heads of Philip's two classical prototypes are engulfed in flames as a portent of their future royal estate. Because the pageant designer wants Philip's portent to appear even greater than theirs, he resists the impulse to make Philip's head also burst forth in flame. As a sign that an imperial—not merely royal—destiny awaits Philip, he invents a greater portent for the prince: a two-headed imperial eagle descends from above to place a garland of laurel on Philip's brow. Such a sight, according to Cornelius Grapheus, the author of the festival book describing this entry, signifies "the *future* power of the Empire."[15] Since the pageant cannot acclaim Philip's imperial advent in the present tense, so to speak—he is, after all, not the present emperor, and, Deo volente, will not be emperor for some time yet—it attempts to read the meaning of Philip's advent in the future conditional: as one of Philip's attendant lords, Calvete de Estrella, puts it, the eagle's descent signifies "the power and dignity of the Imperial estate which the Prince Don Felipe *deserves to have*."[16] If Philip is not the imperial lord who comes at last to his people, perhaps he can be identified as the still expected one who *may* yet come.[17]

Even this prophecy, however, reflects Charles V's hopeful intentions more than Philip's actual status. Although Philip could claim to be the Spanish heir apparent and the heir apparent of the Duke of Brabant, he was not, in fact,

De gheheele
hooghte.lx.
voeten.
De breedde
xxviij.voet.

FIGURE 4. Antwerp Pageant in Koepoortstraat, 1549. Prince Philip, Ascanius, and Servius Tullius manifesting portents of future imperial rule. Grapheus, *La tresadmirable . . . entree,* J6ʳ. By permission of the Folger Shakespeare Library.

the imperial heir apparent except in Charles' mind. In fact, that title belonged to Charles' brother, Ferdinand, King of the Romans, and Ferdinand was clinging tenaciously to the right of succession. One of the chief points of this entry—indeed one of the chief points of the entire imperial progress of which the entry to Antwerp was but the climactic act—was to establish Philip's credentials as a credible pretender to the imperial title so that the electors might be persuaded to set aside Ferdinand's claims and choose Philip instead.[18] As metaphysical theater, then, this pageant is not about Philip at all. Instead of manifesting Philip's newly changed status, an inauguration into imperial dignity, it loyally envisions some *future* imperial inauguration— *if* Charles has his way. It thus offers a vision of Philip as Charles sees him, not necessarily as the people of Antwerp see him. As such, what this pageant design actually stages is an epiphany of Charles V's imperial will.

A number of Antwerp's triumphal arches attempt to present Philip as a worthy and virtuous prince in his own right, but even these suffer considerably from the conceptual awkwardness of the entry. Seen in a booth set into the twelfth of the city's triumphal arches at the Linen Market Square (fig. 5), for instance, seven of Prince Philip's illustrious ancestors present him to Dame Antwerp, who is seated just beneath this royal assembly (G, L4ᵛ–M2ʳ; C, 2:180–81). To the right of Prince Philip stand his Burgundian ancestors: Dukes Philip the Good, Charles the Bold, and Duchess Mary. To the left appear his Habsburg ancestors: Maximilian I, Charles V, and Archduke Philip of Austria. At the same time, a group of three allegorical maidens named Faith, Service, and Sincerity—only two of these appear in the illustration, however—present Dame Antwerp to him.

Since Grapheus tells us that Philip "appears to receive her [i.e., Dame Antwerp] very humanely by the hand," perhaps we are to understand this little scene as an emblem of Philip's formal betrothal to Dame Antwerp.[19] After all, Philip's lordship over Antwerp still lay in the indefinite future, and although he may have sworn an oath to protect the lady's privileges, his symbolic marriage to Dame Antwerp also lay in the future. The pageant thus represents him as the lady's fiancé, but not, I think, her bridegroom. Much might have been made clearer, of course, if the illustrator had chosen to depict the moment in which Philip and Dame Antwerp took one another's hand, but the image itself frankly makes it hard to imagine how the actors performed this little scene: Philip appears holding royal insignia, a sword

De gehee
le hooghte
lrr.voeté.
De breyde
rl.voeten.

FIGURE 5. Antwerp Pageant at the Linen Market Square, 1549. Seven ancestors
present Philip to Dame Antwerp. Grapheus, *La tresadmirable . . . entree,* M2ʳ. By
permission of the Folger Shakespeare Library.

in his right hand and a scepter in his left. Dame Antwerp sits considerably below him. Does she rise from her chair and hold her hand awkwardly upward while Philip drops either his sword or his scepter and stoops even more awkwardly to take her hand? And which hand does each offer the other? If we are to understand the scene in this way, then Philip's Habsburg and Burgundian forebears, together with the people in the streets, necessarily serve as the witnesses to this formal ceremony.[20]

Displays of royal ancestry had long played an important role in the symbolic repertoire of the civic triumph. Throughout the fifteenth and most of the sixteenth centuries, however, representations of the king's ancestry almost always took arboreal form. The joint London entry of Charles V and Henry VIII (1522), for instance, featured a tree rooted in a recumbent figure of John of Gaunt. Its branches displayed some fifty-five "pictures and Images off the parsons off kynges and Quenys and princes all in fyne golde in dyvers setys and stagys and a lyne ascendyng from oon to an other, from the lowest to the hyest." Finally, the top of the tree bloomed forth with "ij ymages one off them representyng the parson off the emprower and another the kynges grace."[21] As this description suggests, such arboreal displays of royal ancestry are iconographical types of Jesse Trees, their trunks rooted in the recumbent form of Jesse, their branches burgeoning with the kings of Israel, and their tops blossoming with images of the Virgin and Child. In royal entries, such trees generally provide the king with a Christ-like messianic genealogy.[22]

In the face of this influential iconographical tradition, however, Antwerp chooses an image of Philip's ancestry that avoids such messianic suggestions. Since Philip could not be depicted as the town's newly inaugurated lord, he could hardly be welcomed as the sacred flower sprung from the Tree of Jesse. As a consequence, these six ancestors merely form themselves into Habsburg and Burgundian wings centered upon the youngest member of the family. The pageant makes no allusion whatsoever to Isaiah's famous prophecy of Christ's birth but merely takes the unremarkable form of an earthly family reunion, even if the family in question is an especially illustrious and important one. Because of their family connections, these family members happily offer themselves as Philip's sponsors and matchmakers. Indeed, as the pageant's legend tells us, their past connection with Dame Antwerp is as important as their family relationship to Philip. Because they have loved, aided, and always advanced the town of Antwerp, they now urge Philip to serve her in the same way. These previous generations of his family offer him avuncular advice; perhaps they serve as witnesses in his formal betrothal, and they certainly provide him with helpful influence in establishing his relationship with Dame Antwerp. The pageant thus represents him as an exceptionally great prince, but a merely human one, and it further undermines any suggestion of Philip's messianic status. A messiah does not require sponsors. He merely manifests his divinity to his faithful people, who then respond in turn by acclaiming his advent.

This pageant occurs amid a number of others, which likewise attempt to recognize Philip's personal virtue and princely status, but in doing so they pointedly refuse to invoke the traditional symbols of messianic kingship. The Antwerp Giant, Druon Antigon (fig. 6), for instance, once held sway over the country that is now Brabant and made himself famous for his cruelty and tyranny (G, K4^v–L2^r; C, 2:108–12, 176–77). Defeated and chained up by Prince Brabon, who founded the Duchy of Brabant, he embodies illegitimate and tyrannical authority forcibly subjected to the legitimate sovereignty of the dukes of Brabant.[23] He makes his reappearance here in the form of a colossal statue which, by mechanical means, rolls its eyeballs, then nods its head as a sign of reverence to Philip. The moment seems tailor-made to serve as a means of recognizing the rightful authority of the new prince. But the giant cannot bow to Philip's rightful authority on this occasion because Philip is not yet the Duke of Brabant. Instead, Druon Antigon's bow of submission only acknowledges Philip's knightly prowess. As the inscription above his head tells us, the giant voluntarily submits himself to Prince Philip because he recognizes a stronger, more powerful hero, one who has the power to defeat him.[24]

If this encounter celebrates Philip's chivalric *virtú*, yet another pageant (fig. 7), erected at St. John's Gate, engages in an allegorical analysis of his personal qualities of character, his inner virtue (G, M2^r–M3^r; C, 2:181–83). Prince Philip stands unmoved while a winged figure of Hope tugs his cloak to our left and a thin, pale, deadly figure of Fear tugs his cloak to our right. Behind him, figures representing Constancy, Confidence, Fortitude, and Magnanimity manifest inner qualities of spirit that enable him to ignore the attempts of Hope and Fear to divert him from his considered course. The various allegorical characters that populate this pageant reflect Philip's

Int Iaer van Tseuentich / met sijn wreet Ghesicht
Heeft den Ruese / ons Coninghe hier me Ghelicht.
CIƆ·IƆ·LXX·Aug.26·

De geheele hoochde lxvij.voetē
De breyde ontrēt .xl. voeten.

ILLE EGO (QVEM FAMA EST, HIS OLIM LOCIS NOVAM
EXERCVISSE TYRANNIDEM) ETSI CORPORIS, &c.

Hier is versupmpt ghe weest hoe dese Kuese had te na dantijke van zijn schouderen hangēde eenen chierlijken scarlakē mantele.

FIGURE 6. The Antwerp Giant, Druon Antigon, 1549. Grapheus, *La tresadmirable . . . entree,* K4ᵛ. By permission of the Folger Shakespeare Library.

De gehee-
le hoochte
lru. voeré.
De brepde
rrrv.voet.

FIGURE 7. Antwerp Pageant at the St. John Gate, 1549. Allegory of Philip's motto, *New Spe Nec Metu*. Grapheus, *La tresadmirable . . . entree,* M3ᵛ. By permission of the Folger Shakespeare Library.

personal motto, "Nec Spe, Nec Metu" (neither by hope nor by fear), and they serve to manifest his princely character: Prince Philip possesses "an heroic strength" that cannot be affected either by hopes of favor or fears of adverse fortune, but always remains fixed on honesty and justice.[25] What is missing, of course, is any suggestion that Philip is invested with the divine gifts that his father had received in the Spanish Merchants' Pageant in Bruges and which made him appear as a type of sacramental kingship. An epiphany of Prince Charles' inner nature had revealed a messiah (fig. 1). Philip, by contrast, is no *christus,* no Anointed One. An epiphany of his inner nature merely reveals an extremely virtuous prince. The pageant certainly stages a memorable manifestation of Philip's personality, but it also studiously avoids making any claims as to Philip's potential role as a sacramental prince.

Perhaps this determined concentration on the personal rather than the sacramental finds its most concrete statement in the immense "Meerbrugge" pageant which stretched for ninety-four feet along the city's main artery (fig. 8). Here an effigy of Philip stands in the center of a group of eight other statues of male figures. Unlike the dynastic pageant we examined earlier, however, this image has nothing to do with Philip's illustrious ancestry. A few of these statues represent members of Philip's family, but most do not. They are all illustrious, but not all of them share Philip's royal status. Two are saints. Remarkably, all eight of these figures share only one characteristic with Prince Philip: his name. They include, according to the pageant narrative, the eight "most virtuous and famous personages or Princes, who have borne the name Philip" or at least the most illustrious ones that the pageant devisers could think of. On Philip's left hand, they include St. Philip the Apostle; King Philip of Spain, the prince's grandfather; Philip the Arabian, first Christian emperor of Rome; and King Philip of Macedon, father of Alexander. On Philip's right hand stand St. Philip the Deacon and three dukes of Burgundy: Philip de Rouvres, Philip the Bold, and Philip the Good.

In its single-minded concern with Philip's illustrious name, this pageant neatly reveals the city's strategy for the reception of a prince who was not their lord but only the heir apparent. The devisers could not very well design the most celebrated imperial festival of the century as if it were a ritual acclamation of Philip's non-existent sacramental lordship, so they designed the show instead as an exercise in extravagant, personal praise. Individually and as a sequence, these pageants follow the dictates of classical rhetoric

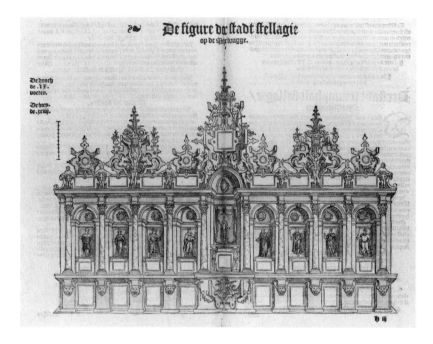

FIGURE 8. Antwerp Pageant at Meerbrugge, 1549. Eight illustrious Philips. Grapheus, *La tresadmirable . . . entree,* H2ᵛ–H3ʳ. By permission of the Folger Shakespeare Library.

rather than those of liturgical worship. Each of the images we have just examined is thus designed about one of the Ciceronian topics of epideictic rhetoric: his name, titles, family, offices, fortune, strength, agility, beauty, and virtues.[26] Accordingly, the pageant makers summon eight Philips to praise his illustrious name; they laud his virtuous character as summed up in his personal motto, "Nec Spe, Nec Metu"; Druon Antigon pays tribute to his power as knight, his chivalric *virtú;* Philip's ancestors appear to demonstrate the greatness of his lineage; as a sign of the prince's fortune, an eagle descends upon his head as witness to his great expectations.

In a civic triumph that was meant to produce a consummate acclamation of support for Philip, we thus find the citizens of Antwerp hedging their bets, so to speak. The pageants freely and generously acknowledge Philip as a worthy and illustrious prince, one deserving of universal praise, but at the same time they qualify and even limit that praise. Above all, they refuse to recognize Philip as their divinely elected prince. In this way, the citizens prudently keep their future options open. They conceive of Philip's advent more in terms of a betrothal ceremony than a marriage, and although betrothals may be legally binding, much might happen before the wedding day. In doing so, however delicately, they suggest the possibility that the ruler's interest and the citizens' interests might differ.

III

In 1582, the citizens of Antwerp again prepared a *joyeuse entrée* for their new duke in circumstances which guaranteed that the divided interests of sovereign and subject would dominate the occasion. Once again, the entry formed part of a progress intended to produce an overwhelming acclamation of loyalty in a difficult situation. Understandably, they built upon their earlier experience, employing redesigned versions of several of the pageants they had first constructed for Prince Philip in 1549. The prince they were inaugurating as Duke of Brabant on this occasion, however, was not Philip of Spain. True, Philip had in fact been formally invested with the sovereignty of the Low Countries in 1555, upon the abdication of Charles V. He saw no need to celebrate a formal *joyeuse entrée* at Antwerp or any other Lowlands city, and when he returned to Spain in 1559, he ruled the provinces thereafter through deputies. By 1577, his policies had failed, and the Netherlands began a determined rebellion against what they increasingly conceived of as Spanish tyranny. As a climactic act in that rebellion, many of the cities of the Netherlands now intended to replace their hereditary sovereign lord with one of their own choosing.[27] As a manifestation of "metaphysical theater," the *joyeuse entrée* of Francis of Anjou into Antwerp thus staged two formal acts at the same time: a renunciation of formal oaths of fealty to Philip and a new act of submission to Anjou. For the first time, a new duke comes to his people not as a king chosen by God for their benefit, but as one chosen by the people for their own benefit. This act of political choice utterly transforms the dynamics of the royal entry. For the first time, the city represents itself as an equally powerful partner of the prince in the newly formed body politic—of the two, perhaps the more powerful partner.

To demonstrate this new, and influential, form of the royal entry, we will examine only the theatrical exchange of oaths that takes place outside

the city of Antwerp and three of the city's pageants. In each of these episodes, the city ignores entirely the traditional representation of the sovereign as a messianic ruler who comes to his people chosen by God. Instead,
as in Philip's triumphal entry of 1549, they recognize him merely for his
splendid personal qualities alone. These qualities, moreover, qualify him for
his new role as Duke of Brabant primarily because they are useful to the
citizens. Furthermore, whereas traditional royal entries had always drama-
tized the power of the messianic prince to transform the city, the Antwerp
entry of 1582, for the first time, dramatizes the power of the city to transform the prince into a sovereign of its own making.

The transforming power of Antwerp begins with the formal acts of
oath taking that would constitute the prince's inauguration. These took place
outside the city walls in a structure especially built for the first epiphany of
the new duke (fig. 9). As the descriptive account of the event puts it, this
building was "a theater erected for the monsieur to shew himselfe vpon to
the people."[28] The town, moreover, had emblazoned a text above the theater which defined the conditional nature of the epiphany that the people of
Antwerp were about to witness:

> O noble prince, whose footsteps faith
>   and gentlenesse preserue:
> Receiue thou here the honour which
>   thy vertue dooth deserue.
>   (H, 4:469)

Whatever the people of Antwerp witness, they will not, therefore, see some
angelic crown descend from on high, perhaps brought to him by angels, as a
sign of messianic sovereignty. Rather, this new duke receives his new dignity
merely as a reward for his virtue. It is, therefore, a gift which the people of
Antwerp have the right to bestow as they choose. Second, the same verses
admonish the new duke to a life of service:

> That these low countries maie at length
>   take breath by meanes of thee,
> And thou a father to vs all
>   in name and dooings bee.
>   (H, 4:469)

FIGURE 9.   Oath-taking Theater outside Antwerp City Gate, 1582. *La Ioyevse &*
magnifique Entree de Monseigneur François, Plate II. By permission of the Research
Library, The Getty Research Institute, Los Angeles.

If the citizens reward Anjou for his virtue with a crown, they will therefore expect him to exercise his formidable powers of virtue on their behalf.

This inaugural theater has also been constructed to show the town of Antwerp to its new governor:

> This theater was set vp towards a corner of the castell, and opened towards the citie, so as his highnesse being there, might at one time view both the citie and the castell, and behold the counterscarffes: the deepe ditches full of faire water cleere to the verie bottome of the chanell, inclosed on either side with hewne stone: the great and faire buildings, the goodlie walles, beautifull to looke on and verie thicke: and the broad rampires garnished wth trees planted by hand, that it resembled a litle forest. (H, 4:469)

To reach this theater, moreover, the duke has had to make his way through "three regiments of the citizens, to the number of a three thousand men in order of battell, who made a goodlie shew with their faire armours and their ensignes displaied." As the Monsieur mounted his theater, they formed their battallions and companies around the stage so that they would be ever present in his sight: "And they neuer went out of their place vntill all the ceremonies were dispatched, and that his highness was gone into the citie" (H, 4:474). Whatever other epiphanies may have taken place that day, the town of Antwerp meant to impress Anjou with the strength of their city and the martial readiness of its citizen army.

In staging the ritual of oath taking in this theater, furthermore, the city emphasizes its power to create its own sovereign. The show begins with an apologia by Monsieur de Hesseils, secretary to the States of Brabant, which consists of a stunning reformation of the theory of the divine election of kings. Because Philip of Spain has violated the rights and liberties of the States of Brabant, the Almighty has explicitly authorized the people of Brabant to appoint a new leader of their own choosing. "Which thing they said could not be better doone than by the election which the said states of Brabant, vnited with the other prouinces, had made of his highnesse person to be their prince and lord, of purpose to bring all things backe to their former order" (H, 4:470–71). Anjou plays his part in this divine plan merely by assenting to the citizens' power to elect him: "mindfull of the honor and good will which they had vouchsafed to yeeld to him, in that among so manie other great princes, they had chosen him out to deliuer them from the oppression and tyrannie of the Spaniards, and to rule them according to their customes, lawes, and priuileges: he thanked them hartilie for it" (H, 4:471).

Throughout this theatrical performance, Anjou only speaks or acts as the States of Brabant feed him his lines or instruct him to move. In swearing to uphold Antwerp's charter of privileges, he thus finds that the charter is written in Dutch, a language he does not understand. As a consequence, the secretary delivers Anjou's lines for him, reading out the oath in Dutch "with a new preface added to the articles, conteining breeflie the reasons and causes of that dealing" (H, 4:471). At the end, Anjou is permitted only a brief declaration of assent. Then like a redeemed sinner in a morality play, he must don new clothes to manifest his transformation in status. The Prince of Orange presents Anjou with the Duke of Brabant's ceremonial "mantle and bonnet of . . . crimosin veluet; the mantle was trailed on the ground, and both of them were furred with powdered ermine turned vp verie brode." Plainly reluctant to put them on, Anjou asks if it is really necessary. The Prince of Orange sternly reminds him of the role he must play: "it behooued him to be apparelled in those robes" for they were "the solemne attire of the princes and dukes of Brabant of old time" (fig. 10). Buttoning the ducal mantle about Anjou's shoulders, the Prince of Orange emphasizes the importance of this unfamiliar costume: "My lord, you must keepe this button fast closed, that no man may pull your mantle from you. And then he set the bonnet vpon his head, and said vnto him: Sir I praie God you may well keepe this attire, for now you may well assure your selfe that you be duke of Brabant" (H, 4:472). Anjou's French countrymen, indeed, seem to have shared their prince's initial reluctance to dress himself in, to them, outlandish Flemish robes. They "woondered to see their master in that apparell, and spake diuerslie of it, as is woont to be doone in matters that are new and erst vnseene." But even they came to see their master in a different light once they understood that these clothes symbolized his new and more exalted identity: "But when they vnderstood how it was the dukelie apparell, and that he wore it as a representation of antiquitie, the like whereof is worne yet still by the electors of the sacred empire in their great ceremonies: they were astonished, and thought him to be a prince of more statelie countenance and maiestie than afore" (H, 4:474).

FIGURE 10.   Anjou dressed in the robes of the Duke of Brabant, 1582. *La Ioyevse &*
magnifique Entree de Monseigneur François, Plate V. By permission of the Research Library,
The Getty Research Institute, Los Angeles.

Retracing Philip of Spain's steps through the city, Anjou found himself confronting Antwerp's old nemesis, Druon Antigon, in Antwerp's great
market square (fig. 11). Moreover, the mechanism had apparently been ad-
justed to permit an even greater act of submission than before. He not only
nods his head toward the new Duke of Brabant, but with one arm he lets
"fall the armes of Spaine which he held in his hand," and with the other he
puts "vp the armes of Aniou." As the verses emblazoned on the table set up
before him tell us, Druon Antigon represents unlawful tyranny:

> Feerce furie, moodie rage, vnbridled ire,
> > Stout force, hot violence, cruell tyrannie,

FIGURE 11.   The Antwerp Giant, Druon Antigon, 1582. *La Ioyevse & magnifique Entree de Monseigneur François,* Plate XI. By permission of the Research Library, The Getty Research Institute, Los Angeles.

> Nought booted me, ne furthered my desire:
> In keeping of my wished souereigntie.
>   (H, 4:478–79)

In 1549, we recall, Philip's encounter with the giant had produced an epiphany of the prince's chivalric *virtú.* The giant's nod paid tribute to a greater and more powerful hero than himself. To understand the nature of Anjou's encounter with the giant, we will have to imagine one feature of the pageant which the engraver has omitted. Whereas Philip of Spain had mastered his Druon Antigon in an otherwise empty square, Anjou encounters the same giant hemmed about by six companies of citizen militia "all in the best armor that was to be seene in anie place of the world" (H, 4:478). The giant is their prisoner, not Anjou's, and if the giant acknowledges Anjou's sovereignty, it is because they permit him to do so. They are the chivalric heroes who have tamed the giant; the scene therefore celebrates their chivalric *virtú,* not Anjou's. Having wrested sovereignty from the giant, the citizens of Antwerp may now award sovereign power to whomever they choose.

This political allegory makes the citizens and their new sovereign partners in defeating Spanish tyranny. If anything, the citizens lay claim to the senior partnership. Anjou does not come to the city to defeat the cruel giant of Spanish tyranny, but he must govern the people justly and keep their conquest safe. Conscious that his own tyranny has been destroyed by the people of Antwerp, Druon Antigon does not hesitate to instruct the new duke in his duties:

> The surest waie for kings to gouerne by,
>> Is mildnesse matched with a prudent mind,
>> To vice seuere, to vertue meeke and kind. . . .
>> By mine example therefore haue a care,
>> All cruell dealings vtterlie to spare.
>
> (H, 4:479)

Perhaps there is even an implicit threat in these lines. The citizen militia have mastered their tyrannous giant once before. Should Anjou adopt the giant's tyranny, then these "imbattled ensignes" stand ready to defeat his tyranny. The citizens who make the duke can unmake him as well.

Antwerp's two most senior chambers of rhetoric—the Goudbloem (Marigold) and the Violieren (Gillyflower)—devised carefully coordinated biblical pageants for Anjou's *joyeuse entrée* that assert even more explicit claims for the power of the citizens to make and unmake their rulers.[29] Both offer episodes from Israel's early history as parallels to Anjou's advent. Since both pageants explicitly quote scripture from the Book of Samuel (as it is known in most Reformed biblical translations) rather than the Book of Kings (as it is known in the Vulgate), the devisers take pains to portray Antwerp as a community dominated by Reformed churches. Furthermore, both pageants explicitly emphasize the religious differences that separate Antwerp from its new duke, who remained a Roman Catholic.

The first of these pageants (fig. 12), which was contributed by the "Souci" chamber,[30] portrays in its three compartments how God replaced Saul with David as King of Israel. In the left-hand compartment, Samuel charges Saul with disobedience to God and rends a piece of his cloak from him "in token that the kingdome should be plucked from Saules house and giuen to a better." In the middle compartment, God chooses David as Israel's new king from among the sons of Jesse. In the right-hand compartment, David, now anointed by God, slays Goliath. For the most part, of course, the pageant offers a straightforward parallel to the citizens' election of Anjou to replace the tyrannous Philip of Spain. As the legend emblazoned above the theater puts it,

> As God bereauing Saule of crowne and mace,
>   Did dispossesse him of his kingdome quight,
> And after set vp Dauid in his place:
>   So now likewise dispatching from our sight,
> The tyrans which oppressed vs by might,
>   He giueth thee (o noble duke) the reine
> Of these our countries, ouer vs to reine.
>
> (H, 4:476–77)

God's election of Anjou, the pageant foresees, will allow him to slay the giant of Spanish tyranny. But at the same time the threat of dispossession can also apply to Anjou as much as it once applied to Philip. William of Orange might well have been preparing Anjou for this scene as he clothed the new duke in his ceremonial mantle and bonnet. If Anjou recalled William's cryptic remarks, this scene would give them new meaning: "My lord, you must keepe this button fast closed, that no man may pull your mantle from you. . . . Sir I praie God you may well keepe this attire, for now you may well assure your selfe that you be duke of Brabant" (H, 4:472).

The second of these biblical stages (fig. 13), devised by the Violieren chamber,[31] offers an even more striking biblical parallel for the city's claim to equal status with its new duke. Under the title, "Knit together by singlenesse,"[32] the pageant design summons up "the neere aliance of Dauid and

FIGURE 12. Pageant designed by the Souci Chamber of Rhetoric, 1582. God replaces Saul as King of Israel. *La Ioyevse & magnifique Entree de Monseigneur François,* Plate VI. By permission of the Research Library, The Getty Research Institute, Los Angeles.

FIGURE 13.   Pageant designed by the Violier Chamber of Rhetoric, 1582. The "Near Alliance" of David and Jonathas. *La Ioyevse & magnifique Entree de Monseigneur François,* Plate VII. By permission of the Research Library, The Getty Research Institute, Los Angeles.

Ionathas, to betoken the firmenesse of the oth mutuallie made by his highnes and the states of Brabant." On the stage, the cardinal virtues gather around David (identified by his crown) and Jonathan, who are shaking hands while Dame Antwerp presides over the gathering. The scene seems to offer a straightforward biblical parallel for the new relationship that Anjou has just entered into with the States of Brabant—until, that is, we notice the rather dizzying turn in meaning that these symbols have taken. We expect that Anjou will once again find himself represented in David, the anointed king and slayer of giants; the States of Brabant, surely, must find themselves represented in Jonathan, David's fast friend and "near ally." In fact, however, the pageant chooses to reverse these symbols. As the legend above the scene informs us, *Anjou* is instead here symbolized by "the faithfull Ionathas" who "did promise to defend, / Good Dauid from the harmes which Saule / against him did intend." Symbolized in David, the States expect that Anjou, like Jonathan, will defend them "Against the tyrans by whose force / we haue beene sore opprest" (H, 4:477).

I know of no earlier pageant in the entire history of the royal entry that permits the citizens to cast themselves so forcefully in the role that has always been reserved for messianic kings. For the first time in the history of the form, as far as I know, the citizens stake their own claim to be mediators of God's grace. We began this study by examining an image dating from the early years of the sixteenth century, which depicts the prince as the Anointed One and claims for him the divine power to transform an earthly city into a type of the holy city of Jerusalem. Here, toward the end of the century, the citizens have claimed that role. They now represent themselves as anointed by the grace of God, and they now claim, for the first time, the Godlike power to make men into kings.

NOTES

1. While none of the towers of the pageant image depict actual buildings, their architecture is nonetheless strongly reminiscent of such Bruges structures as the Halle tower and the Belfort, with its octagonal lantern. For a convenient collection of contemporaneous views of Bruges, especially the later sixteenth-century view of Bruges as a city of towers, see Valentin Vermeersch, *Bruges* (Antwerp: Mercatorfonds, 2002), 92–93.

2. For a discussion of this image, see Gordon Kipling, *Enter the King: Theatre, Liturgy, and Ritual in the Medieval Civic Triumph* (Oxford: Clarendon Press, 1998), 121–22.

3. Most readers will recognize my borrowing of this term from Clifford Geertz, who observes that in the culture of the late Middle Ages, images like this have the power to embody, through theatrical representation, an ideal of political order. Further, Geertz would argue, by entering together into a theatrical representation of an ideal political order, king and citizens attempt to shape the existing conditions of their lives into the pattern defined by the theatrical representation. The culture so preoccupied with transforming the real into the ideal by means of theatrical representation is what Geertz would call the "Theatre State." See *Negara: The Theatre State in Nineteenth-Century Bali* (Princeton, NJ: Princeton University Press, 1980), 13, 104.

4. Du Puys' text exists in two versions: (1) an illustrated presentation manuscript, once in the collection of Charles' sister, Marie of Hungary: Vienna, Österreichische Nationalbibliothek, Cod. 2591; (2) a printed text with woodcut illustrations similar to the illustrations in the manuscript version: *La tryumphante et solemnelle entree . . . de treshault trespuissant et tresexcellent prince Monsieur Charles prince des hespaignes Archiduc daustrice duc de bourgongne . . . En sa ville de Bruges lan mil. V. cēs &. Xv. Le xviiiᵉ iour dapuril apres Pasques* (Paris: Gilles de Gourmont, 1515). For a discussion of the relationship between these two texts and between the manuscript and woodcut illustrations, see Sydney Anglo, ed., *La tryumphante Entree de Charles Prince des Espagnes en Bruges 1515* (Amsterdam: Theatrvm Orbis Terrarvm [1973]), 7–11. Properly speaking, du Puys did not produce "the earliest printed description of a royal entry" (Anglo, *La tryumphante Entree*, 6), but it was certainly the first printed and illustrated one. The earliest printed description known to me is *Lētree faicte A paris par trespuissant prince & seigneur / Larcheduc de austriche / Conte de flandres* (Paris, 1501), but there may have been others. As an example of a later "quotation" from du Puys' text, compare his illustration and description of the pageant of Orpheus with a very similar pageant designed for the entry of Philip of Spain into London in 1554, for which see Robert Withington, *English Pageantry,* 2 vols. (Cambridge, MA: Harvard University Press, 1918–26), 1:192–93.

5. Roy Strong, *Art and Power: Renaissance Festivals, 1450–1650* (Berkeley and Los Angeles: University of California Press, 1984), 89. For the most substantial modern commentaries on this important ritual spectacle, see W. Kuyper in *The Triumphant Entry of Renaissance Architecture into the Netherlands,* 2 vols. (Alphen aan den Rijn: Canaletto, 1994) and especially Mark A. Meadow, "Ritual and Civic Identity in Philip II's 1549 Antwerp *Blijde Inkompst,*" *Nederlands Kunsthistorisch Jaarboek* 49 (1998): 36–67.

6. Charles was clearly interested in consolidating power throughout the empire and in transmitting as much of that power as possible to his son, Philip. The Netherlands formed a particularly difficult challenge to these centralizing motives

because the provinces had no political unity beyond their allegiance to a common ruler. He ruled Brabant as Duke of Brabant, Holland as the Count of Holland, Flanders as the Count of Flanders, and so on. Under these conditions, the purpose of the entry into Antwerp—indeed, the common purpose of the entries into the major cities of all the provinces of the Netherlands—was to secure Philip's position as Charles' heir, and by so doing further the cause of imperial consolidation. For the purposes of Philip's imperial progress, see Henry Kamen, *Philip of Spain* (New Haven, CT: Yale University Press, 1997), 34–45. The imperial progress that brought Philip to the Netherlands began in Italy and passed through the German states before reaching the Low Countries. By arranging Philip's triumphal progress through virtually all of his domains, Charles was clearly attempting to establish Philip's credentials as a potential universal ruler. This act of imperial representation was necessary because Charles' brother, Ferdinand, was King of the Romans and thus the heir apparent to the imperial crown. The pageants themselves are really not much concerned with Philip as the future ruler of the Low Countries. Rather, they repeatedly anticipate "the power and dignity of the Imperial estate which the Prince Don Felipe deserves to have" (see below, n. 16).

7. For the purposes of this essay, I limit my commentary to those pageants designed by the city of Antwerp. There are fourteen of these in all, including the appearance of the Antwerp Giant, Druon Antigon. Except where otherwise specified, I cite details of the Antwerp triumph of 1549 from the two following texts: (1) Cornelius Grapheus, *La tresadmirable, tresmagnifique, & triumphante entree, du treshault & trespuissant Prince Philipes, Prince d'Espaignes, filz de Lempereur Charles. v^c., ensemble la vraye description des Spectacles, theatres, archz triumphaulx .&c. lesquelz ont este faictz & bastis a sa tresdesiree reception en la tresnommee florissante ville dAnuers. Anno 1549* (Antwerp: Pierre Gillis van Diest for Pierre Coeck d'Allost, 1550); and (2) Juan Cristóbal Calvete de Estrella, *El Felicísimo Viaje del Muy Alto Y Muy Poderoso Príncipe don Felipe,* 2 vols. (Madrid: Sociedad de Bibliófilos Españoles, 1930), 2:108–17. The apotheosis pageant can be found on fols. N2^r–N3^v in Grapheus and on 2:189–91 in Calvete de Estrella. Future references will be cited in the text, thus: G, N2^r–N3^v and C, 2:189–91.

8. Meadow, taking a very different view of this pageant image to the one I propose here, argues that it was "entirely dedicated to flattering Philip" ("Ritual and Civic Identity," 60).

9. The citizens of Antwerp clearly attempted to create an entry that would outshine all others. The extraordinary series of books, intended to preserve the city's accomplishments for posterity, offers convincing evidence of this motive. These books, with a text by Cornelius Grapheus, were published in three languages— Latin, French, and Dutch—and consisted of both illustrated and non-illustrated versions. The woodcuts of the illustrated versions were designed by Pieter Coecke van Aelst, and many of these illustrated editions circulated in de luxe, hand-colored versions. For these various texts, see John Landwehr, *Splendid Ceremonies: State En-*

tries and Royal Funerals in the Low Countries, 1515–1791, A Bibliography (Nieuwkoop: B. De Graaf, and Leiden: A. W. Sijthoff, 1971), 73–75.

10. For the constitutional purposes of the *joyeuse entrée,* see Bruce D. Lyon, "Fact and Fiction in English and Belgian Constitutional Law," *Medievalia et humanistica* 10 (1956): 82–101; Kipling, *Enter the King,* 39–40.

11. As both Meadow ("Ritual and Civic Identity," 40–41) and Kuyper (*Triumphant Entry of Renaissance Architecture,* 1:12) point out, Charles and Philip enter a specially constructed temple at the boundary of the city where Philip swore an oath of some kind. Calvete de Estrella reports that the prince swore an oath merely to defend the Church, after which representatives of the civic establishment swear allegiance to him and receive him as "legítimo sucesor del Marquesado del Sacro Imperio con cierta solenidad y cerimonia, que tienen desde el tiempo antiguo" (*El Felicísimo Viaje,* 2:196–97). Meadow thinks that Calvete mistakes the nature of the oath and that it "was in fact a specific promise to respect all the rights and privileges of Antwerp, as well as a reconfirmation of the *blijde inkomst* to which he had sworn [several weeks] earlier in Leuven." While this interpretation is far from certain, the mere swearing to (or even signing of) the oath does not make Philip the sovereign Duke of Brabant at this time, although it may mean that he will not have to repeat the oath when, some years later, he does succeed his father as duke. To enter this inaugural temple, Philip passes through an arch specifically devoted to celebrating Philip's accession as Marquis of the Holy Roman Empire. The initial oath-taking ceremony at the boundary of the city of Antwerp thus seems limited specifically to his inauguration as marquis, which is how the citizens seem to have interpreted it.

12. According to Grapheus, Philip went to a large room in the Maison de la ville on the day after the entry. There he met with an assembly of great personages, noble seigneurs, masters of the law of the town, and representatives of the commons. The ensuing ceremony confirmed him as Charles' *"futur* successeur hereditaire" to great, popular acclamation. The ceremony thus merely acknowledged the status he already possessed; it did not inaugurate him into a new one (*La tresadmirable . . . entree,* N3ᵛ). Because Antwerp was a marquisate of the empire, however, Philip did indeed become the city's lord, but only in a subordinate sense. As a marquis, he ranked below a duke, and he thus remained—as he always had been—subordinate to his father both as Duke of Brabant and as Holy Roman Emperor. For these reasons, perhaps, neither Antwerp nor any other Lowlands city had ever before thought to mark a prince's investiture to this dignity significant enough to require a *joyeuse entrée.* Nor would this experiment ever be repeated in the future. For a different interpretation of this ceremony, see Meadow, "Ritual and Civic Identity," 61, in which he reads, mistakenly in my view, the "officials of Antwerp" recognizing Philip as "our future, certain and undoubted Lord, here present as Duke of Brabant and Margrave of the Holy Roman Empire." To my mind, a crucial comma (represented by a virgule in the original text, see p. 67 n. 69) has been omitted after "here present," which has the effect of making the officials recognize Philip here and now as both

duke and marquis when all that they mean, I think, is that they recognize that their *future* duke is now "here present" before them.

13. "Alcides, Atlasqve ingens, nvgae omnia, vere isti hvmeris gestant totivs pondera mvndi" (Calvete de Estrella, *El Felicísimo Viaje,* 2:179).

14. Kuyper observes in this respect that "legally the whole entry was meant for Philip, so it is striking that the general tone is far friendlier towards Charles than to Philip. Partly this was the result of formality; the *joyeuse entrée* while the subject of the former *blijde inkomst* was still head of state. This provoked comparison which by their very nature must be less flattering or at least mildly intriguing to Philip" (*Triumphant Entry of Renaissance Architecture,* 1:76).

15. "Mais nostre Prince sur son chief descēdoit vng aigle, a deux chiefz, tenāt en sa griffe vne grāde branche de laurier, signifiant (selon la pensee anticque des Rommains) la puissance future de l'Empire" (Grapheus, *La tresadmirable . . . entree,* I4ᵛ).

16. "Tenía sobre su cabeça una águila, como que volaba suavemente con un ramo de laurel; *significaba la potestad y dignidad del Imperio que el Príncipe Don Felipe merece tener*" (*El Felicísimo Viaje,* 2:166). My italics.

17. I have not been able to address here the neoclassicism of this entry. The innovative and explicitly Roman architecture of this entry reflects precisely Charles V's determination that his son should be seen as heir to the Holy Roman Empire. For an important and provocative analysis of the Serlian architecture of this entry, see Meadow, "Ritual and Civic Identity," 49–52. Kuyper, as the title of his study *The Triumphant Entry of Renaissance Architecture into the Netherlands* suggests, thinks of this entry as both innovative and seminal in establishing neoclassical architecture in the Netherlands.

18. Roy Strong appears mistaken in thinking that "the Antwerp entry was a scaled-down celebration of a political failure. It had been planned to welcome Philip as the next emperor, but the refusal of the Electors to grant Charles's wish meant that Philip entered Antwerp only as a future king of Spain and as Marquess of the Holy Roman Emperor in Antwerp" (*Art and Power,* 89). The Antwerp festivities may have fallen short of the city's extremely ambitious intentions in some respects, but the politics of the imperial succession had nothing to do with it. Nearly a year *after* the Antwerp entry (July 1550), Charles summoned an Imperial Diet at Augsburg to debate the succession, among other matters. The matter was not formally settled until 9 March 1551, when Charles yielded to the determined opposition of his brother and nephew and decreed that the imperial crown would pass first to his brother Ferdinand, then to Philip, then to Ferdinand's son, Maximilian. For these negotiations, see Kamen, *Philip of Spain,* 45–48. Kuyper discusses the role of this Antwerp triumph in Charles V's campaign to establish Philip as his imperial successor in *Triumphant Entry of Renaissance Architecture,* 1:7–9, 74–78.

19. "Icy voioit on, que Fides, Candor, & Obsequentia, prendoient Antuerpia par la main, & le presentoient treshumblement a nostre Prince Philipes, quy sembloit

la recepuoir treshumainement de la main, aussy sembloit que trous yeulx aultres personnaiges luy monstroient ioieuse chiere" (*La tresadmirable . . . entree,* M1ᵛ).

20. Initially, Meadow thought that Grapheus meant this scene to be an emblem of Philip's ritual marriage with the city ("Ritual and Civic Identity," 47), but in a later article he remarks, more correctly in my view, that "the iconography of this tableau is clearly that of a betrothal between Antwerp and Philip" ("'Met Geschicter Ordenen': The Rhetoric of Place in Philip II's 1549 Antwerp Blijde Incompst," *Journal of the Walters Art Gallery* 57 [1999], 3). For the imagery of the nuptial or betrothal handclasp (*dextrarum iunctio*) and the iconography of both marriage and betrothal scenes, see Edwin Hall, *The Arnofini Betrothal: Medieval Marriage and the Enigma of Van Eyck's Double Portrait* (Berkeley: University of California Press, 1994), 67–79.

21. Cambridge, Corpus Christi College, MS 298 (no. 8), 136. See Kipling, *Enter the King,* 64.

22. Some royal entries explicitly make this typological point by erecting two such trees side by side—Christ's Jesse Tree on the one hand, and the king's royal tree on the other. A London pageant for Henry VI (1432), for example, placed a Jesse Tree showing Christ's descent from Jesse in typological opposition to a genealogical tree showing Henry's descent from Saints Edward and Louis (John Lydgate, *Minor Poems,* ed. H. N. MacCracken, EETS o.s. 192, 2 [London: Oxford University Press, 1934], 643–44). On the subject of Jesse Tree pageants in royal entries generally, see Kipling, *Enter the King,* 63–71.

23. On the subject of giants in the foundation myths of cities, see Walter B. Stephens, *Giants in Those Days: Folklore, Ancient History, and Nationalism* (Lincoln: University of Nebraska Press, 1989), and Victor I. Scherb, "Assimilating Giants: The Appropriations of Gog and Magog in Medieval and Early Modern England," *Journal of Medieval and Early Modern Studies* 32 (2002): 59–84.

24. "Ille ego, qvem fama est, his olim locis novam exercvisse tyrannidem, et si corporis vastitate adhvc dvm sim formidabilis posita iam feritate tibi Philippe Princeps Max. libens cedo, tvaeqve me potestati vltro svbiicio." As Grapheus points out, this scripture is written "en maniere cõme sy le giant eusse parle" (*La tresadmirable . . . entree,* L1ᵛ. Latin scripture text from Calvete de Estrella, *El Felicísimo Viaje,* 2:177).

25. According to Calvete de Estrella, this pageant "daban a entender que el generoso ánimo del Príncipe así ha de ser confirmado de una heroica fortaleza, que por ninguna causa, por ningunos efetos, por ningunas esperanças de favor o provecho, o de cosas prósperas se incline a la una parte, ni menos por miedo de daños de la adversa fortuna, o de otras cualesquier perturbaciones o adversidades se tuer ça a la otra parte de lo honesto y justo, y de la igualdad que se debe tener en la vida, antes estando firme sobre la piedra cuadrada, que de su natural nunca cae, esté constante para todas las cosas que pueden suceder, sin inclinarse, ni a la una, ni a la otra mano" (*El Felicísimo Viaje,* 2:183). In this passage, he elaborates on a similar description in Grapheus, *La tresadmirable . . . entree,* M3ʳ.

26. For the topics of epideictic rhetoric, see Cicero, *De Inventione,* 1:24.35—36, and the pseudo-Ciceronian *Rhetorica ad Herennium,* 3.6—8, perhaps the most popular of the "Ciceronian" rhetorics in the sixteenth century. They were divided into three categories: external circumstances, physical attributes, and qualities of character. See in particular Harry Caplan's introduction to his Loeb Classical Library edition (London: William Heinemann, 1964), li—liv.

27. For the political background to this entry, see H. M. C. Purkis' "Introduction" to her edition of *La magnifique Entrée de François d'Anjou en sa ville d'Anvers* (Amsterdam: Theatrvm Orbis Terrarvm [1973]), 7—15 [Landwehr 44]; Henri Pirenne, *Histoire de la Belgique,* 4 (Brussels, 1911); Frances A. Yates, *The Valois Tapestries,* 2nd ed. (London: Routledge & Kegan Paul, 1975). Illustrations taken from the Getty copy of the original, *La Ioyevse & magnifique Entree de Monseigneur Françoys, Fils de France, et Frere Vnicque du Roy, par la grace de Dieu, Dvc de Brabant, d'Anjou, Alençon, Berri, &c. En sa tres-renommée ville d'Anvers* (Antwerp: Christophle Plantin, 1582).

28. Raphael Holinshed, *Chronicles of England, Scotland, and Ireland,* 6 vols. (London, 1808), 4:469. Holinshed includes a contemporary English translation of *La magnifique Entrée* in his text which he titles, "The Roiall Interteinement of the Right High and Mightie Prince, Francis the French Kings Onelie Brother, By the Grace of God Duke of Brabant, Aniou, Alanson, Berrie, &c, into the Citie of Antwerpe" (4:466—88). I will generally quote from this source. Future citations will be identified in the text, thus: H, 4:469.

29. Antwerp also had a third chamber of rhetoric, the "olijftak" (Olive Branch), but it was the two senior chambers that "over the course of the late fifteenth and sixteenth centuries" most energetically "vied with each other to bring the greatest glory to their community." In providing these pageants, the chambers were performing one of their expected tasks. The charter of the Gillyflower chamber, for instance, "enjoined its companions to perform plays, entertainments, and allegorical riddles (*zinnebeeldische raedsels*) or refrains 'to the entertainment of the community,' and to present to the audience the question or topic of the performance in the form of a large banner of blazon. Moreover, like rhetoricians elsewhere, the Gillyflower's actors were expected to participate in various rhetorician competitions and to bring home their share of prizes for the promotion of the city" (Gary K. Waite, *Reformers on Stage: Popular Drama and Religious Propaganda in the Low Countries of Charles V, 1515—1556* [Toronto: University of Toronto Press, 2000], 51—52).

30. *La magnifique Entrée* assigns this pageant to the Antwerp chamber of rhetoric, "le Soussi, ou cõme aucuns l'appellẽt le Sol-suit, pour estre vne fleur suiuant le Soleil: & ladite chãbre a pour sa deuise *Accroissant en vertu*" (D2ʳ). As the French writer points out, the chamber was named for its emblem, the "Souci," or "Sol-suit," i.e., the Marigold ("tournesol" in French, "goudbloem" in Dutch). It was the second oldest of Antwerp's chambers of rhetoric, originating in the late fifteenth century shortly after the emergence of the Violieren Society (for which seen n. 31 below). See Waite, *Reformers on Stage,* 52—53. Holinshed's literal translation mistakenly renders the name

of the chamber as "Care" (derived from another meaning of the French "souci"), accurately describes its emblem as "Followsun," and only slightly mistranslates its motto as "Growing up in vertue" (H, 4:476). For the Antwerp chambers in general, see Waite, *Reformers on Stage,* 51–78.

31. *La magnifique Entrée* refers to this chamber as "vne autre Chambre des Rhetoriciens appellez les Peintres ou Violiers ayans pour leur deuise *Par candeur assemblez*" (D3ʳ). The "Violieren," Antwerp's first rhetorician society, was "officially created out of St Luke's artist guild" in 1480, and both guilds continued to share the same "device" or motto: "wt Jonsten versaemt" (Dutch) or "par candeur assemblez" (French): "gathered in goodwill." The rhetoricians took as their emblem the "Violier" (i.e., the Wallflower or Gillyflower), although Holinshed apparently does not recognize the English equivalent, so he does not risk a translation (H, 4:477). In 1504, the Violieren achieved "the status of one of the city's 'sworn' or 'privileged' guilds, those that directly served the city, such as the various ceremonial guard, marksmen guilds, and confraternities" (Waite, *Reformers on Stage,* 51–52). George Kernodle mistakenly refers to it as the "Society of the Violet" (*From Art to Theatre* [Chicago: University of Chicago Press, 1944], 111–29). The Violieren Society had a reputation for moderate Protestantism and numbered Lutherans among its leaders. In the 1539 rhetoricians' competition at Ghent, Jan van den Berghe's explicitly Lutheran play won the prize for the Antwerp Violieren, and as Waite points out, "no reprimand was forthcoming from either the Ghent or Antwerp authorities for the Gillyflower's 1539 award-winning play" (Waite, *Reformers on Stage,* 70; see also Waite's discussion of the Antwerp rhetoricians' engagements with the Reformation generally, pp. 51–78).

32. This is Holinshed's rather awkward literal translation of the Violieren Society's motto (above, n. 31).

The Eye of the Procession

Ritual Ways of Seeing in the Renaissance

EDWARD MUIR

Allow me to invite you to look again at a familiar image, Pieter Bruegel the Elder's *The Fight between Carnival and Lent* (1559, fig. 1). The painting's visual bustle betrays an encyclopedic character that is Rabelaisian in its amplitude, cataloguing a wide variety of popular games, celebrating holiday foods and drink, and allegorizing the cosmic struggle between the festive period of Carnival on the left side, which celebrates the pleasures of the flesh, and the liturgical season of Lent on the right, which extols pious self-control.[1]

In the foreground of Bruegel's painting two ill-formed processions are about to meet headlong in a joust with makeshift spears, one wielded by a corpulent personification of Carnival and the other by a bony Lent. A considerable body of scholarship has been devoted to identifying the iconographic markers in Bruegel's masterwork—the crow-meat pie on King Carnival's head, his coat-of-arms ham, Lent's long-handled paddle-lance adorned with two scraggly fish, and the pretzels at his feet—but I want to emphasize something else: how the painting has been structured around two processions.[2] Bruegel's decision to represent the dichotomies of human life in these processional forms reveals a predisposition not just to represent cultural topoi through iconography, so typical

FIGURE I. Pieter Bruegel, the Elder, *Fight between Carnival and Lent* (1559).
Kunsthistorisches Museum, Vienna. Photo credit: Erich Lessing / Art Resource, NY.

of medieval and Renaissance artists, but also to imagine society as structured through public rituals, especially through the kinesics of public processions.

The constructed dynamics of processions created ritual-specific ways of seeing, which can be described as follows. First, contemporary optical theories suggested that the viewers of rituals were brought under the influence of what they saw through a profusion of material or spiritual emanations or, to put it in their terms, through the radiation of species. A ritual, especially an ecclesiastical or official procession, attempted to irradiate viewers with beneficent spiritual or authoritarian influences. One of the sources of the reputed capacity of public processions to create social harmony, therefore, was their ability to maximize the radiation of beneficial species broadly throughout the troubled atmosphere of the community.

Second, the spectators of a procession were simultaneously being viewed by those who marched in the procession so that the seeing subject and seen object were, in fact, interchangeable. Much more significantly than a liturgical celebration at the altar or a baptism at the font, a procession through the streets of a town blurred the subject/object distinction, which is also one of the sources for processions' dangerous social potential to metamorphose from ritual order to ritual riot.[3] Spectators in the act of spectating became just as much a part of the procession as the processors themselves, and the mutual influences between processors and spectators produced by sight created an improvisational unpredictability in processions.

Third, the kinetic character of rituals, which were effectively improvisations on a loose script, makes it impossible to affix a single meaning to a specific ritual performance. Rituals created a peculiar oxymoron: they were performances that always varied from one repetition to another but that attempted to mask variation by asserting their unchanging character. They are examples of "invented traditions" par excellence, and the late medieval and Renaissance obsession with codifying rituals through the appointment of ritual managers, such as heralds and masters of ceremony, and the writing up of prescriptive texts, the Books of Ceremonies, testifies to the anxiety created by ritual kinesis.[4] The explosion of theological, reformist, and apologetic discussions of ritual during the sixteenth century, in particular, further suggests a widespread unease with the ambiguity of meaning in rituals.[5] I wish to suggest that the struggle to affix a consistent meaning to ritual was a vain quest because it is the very defiance of uniform meaning while evoking powerful emotions that produces the lure of ritual.

Processions were, of course, not synonymous with ritual, that vast range of formal repetitive behaviors found in liturgies, festivals, and rites of passage. But, as Arnold van Gennep recognized more than a century ago, all rituals might be best understood as rites of passage from one biological, spiritual, seasonal, social, or political state to another.[6] Processions acted out an urban rite of passage—those who paraded in them and the objects they carried moved from one place to another, often from a church into the streets of the city, bringing what was normally hidden in a tabernacle, or framed on an altar, or housed in a reliquary into the public open spaces of the city and then returning the object to its home. Processions, moreover, diminished, to use van Gennep's language, the preliminary rite of separation and the post-liminary rite of incorporation to extend and emphasize the liminary rite of transition. A procession was, in effect, a mobile and extended threshold between one social state and another, an especially powerful mechanism for bringing the sacred to the laity. A procession contrasted with baptism, for example, which emphasized the other stages of a rite of passage: the separation of the infant from its natal family and its reincorporation into the Christian community while the actual liminal moment was the brief one when the priest dipped or sprinkled the baby with the baptismal water. A procession, then, should be understood as a state of prolonged liminality.

What does sight have to do with the social processes enacted by rituals? Or, to put the question more precisely, *how* did people see during processions, *what* did they see in processions, and how did people *understand* what they saw? Before we explore these questions, a crucial qualification about the nature of the representation of rituals should be kept in mind. Although this essay will discuss a number of images that repute to represent actual ritual performances and will rely on a number of texts that supposedly describe rituals, we cannot, it should be obvious, directly observe a medieval or Renaissance ritual. The object of study here is neither an image nor a text but an event that took place at a particular time and place. All we have to examine are footprints in the snow, signs that some animal we have chosen to call a "ritual" once passed by. The footprints we have left are mere traces of that animal and can be found in paintings, engravings, musical scores, prescriptive and descriptive texts, and criminal records from cases of rituals that turned violent. These images and texts followed their own rules of composition and evoked their own representational traditions, just as rituals did, but those rules and traditions were different from those that operated in ritual performances. I emphasize the simple fact that there is no actual ritual text to read or actual ritual representation to interpret because one must never confuse the static visual representations or textual prescriptions or descriptions of rituals for that now long lost dynamic moment of a particular ritual performance. In the case of processions, moreover, no one observer ever knew the whole because a procession required many participants who typically improvised what they actually did from a loosely defined ceremonial script, and the procession changed as it passed from one place to another. A procession created the same epistemological conundrum as the water in a river, always passing by, never actually the same water, but we choose to see the river as a unified phenomenon and labeled with a name—the river Arno—as a way of making it possible to talk about it.[7]

All medieval or Renaissance processions, no matter how elaborate or pompous, derived from the archetypical ecclesiastical procession in which ritual specialists, such as a priest, bishop, or confraternity member, carried a sacral object, such as the host, a relic, or a miraculous image, with the objective of bringing the object into the view of those who watched the procession. An exemplary representation can be found in Gentile Bellini's *Procession on the Piazza San Marco* (fig. 2) in Venice, in which the members of the confraternity parade their most valued relic through the piazza and are followed by the senior political officials of the republic, here visually subordinated by their relegation to the periphery on the far right side of the painting.

The sacred object takes pride of place in the visual center of the painting, just as it did by its location in the center of the procession itself.[8] Processions such as these are prime examples of what Peter Brown has argued is the distinctively Christian notion of the mobility of the sacred.[9] Instead of sacred places, medieval Christians oriented worship around sacred objects, most notably the eucharistic body of Christ and the remains of the dead. From this point of view, medieval Christianity is fundamentally a cult of the dead, and as Craig Koslofsky has shown, the Protestant Reformation can be fruitfully interpreted as a revolt against the demands the dead placed on the living through obligatory ritual services, such as masses for the dead, costly tombs, extended funerals, and the celebration of saints' cults.[10]

A variation on the root ecclesiastical procession required processors to walk by a sacral object which remained in the fixed location. It does not seem to have been a crucial consideration whether the sacred object was itself mobile or whether those who viewed it were mobile, in effect conducting a kind of local pilgrimage through the streets of the city. In other words, the procession could either maximize the number of viewers of the sacred by moving a sacred object through the streets of the city or the viewers might form a procession to pass by the sacred object while it remained in a fixed place.

In Siena priests carried icons of the Virgin, the patron saint of the city, in processions on her feast days, and Siena's prosperous and pious citizens so craved to honor the Virgin that the city government commissioned ever more elaborate panels. It is unclear, at least to me, at what point the panels became so large that the processions shifted from a progress through the

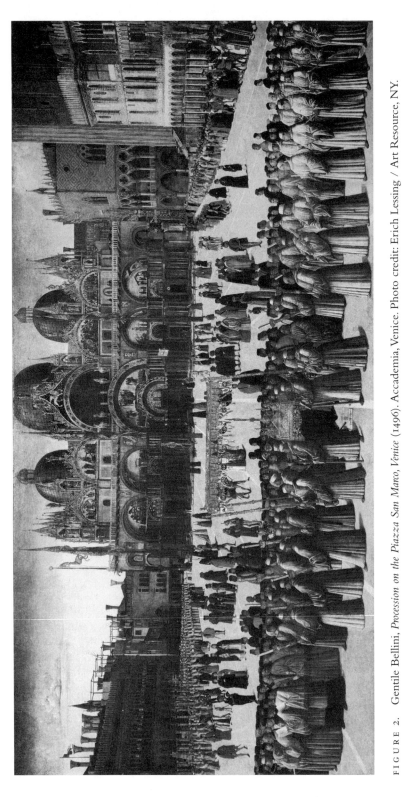

FIGURE 2. Gentile Bellini, *Procession on the Piazza San Marco, Venice* (1496). Accademia, Venice. Photo credit: Erich Lessing / Art Resource, NY.

street with the image to one in which the Sienese filed past an image that was left in place in the cathedral. That was certainly the case after 1308 when in fulfillment of one of these commissions Duccio painted the grand *Maestà,* which is about six feet high by twelve feet wide and thus too large to be picked up and carried through the streets of the city. The *Maestà* became the altarpiece for the high altar in Siena's cavernous cathedral, and in the statutes dated between 1337 and 1339 (which repeated earlier statutes on this point) all male residents of the city between the ages of eighteen and seventy were required on the eve of the feast of the Assumption of the Virgin to process into the cathedral, pass by the *Maestà,* and make candle offerings to her. On the feast of the Assumption proper delegates from subject towns made their own pilgrimage to the cathedral where they offered legally prescribed amounts of candle wax. Only certain categories of criminals were exempt from the candle offerings. The Sienese authorities experimented with variant kinds of processions that maximized the number of people who saw the sacred image of the Madonna, and these authorities seemed to understand that the image must be seen to exercise her beneficent influences. The Sienese obsession with the Virgin was such that they exported her to the countryside where versions of the *Maestà* type proliferated in subject villages and allied towns.[11]

The procession to an image or shrine, of course, became a means for institutionalizing the pilgrimage. These two processional models of carrying a sacred image or processing past one could be combined as in this Corpus Christi procession in early seventeenth-century Venice (fig. 3). Processors carried the body of Christ and floats displaying scenes and inscriptions designed to indoctrinate the population. This procession, however, continued from the public space of the piazza into the private chapel of the doge, the Basilica of San Marco, where processors walked in front of the *Pala d'Oro,* an elaborately enameled and jeweled panel mounted behind the high altar. After the formal procession passed through the piazza, spectators followed into the church also to view the *Pala,* which was kept hidden except on special feast days. Richard Trexler has demonstrated how there was a kind of sacred economy at work in these processions.[12] Outside Florence the *Madonna of Impruneta,* for example, was normally kept covered so that the force of her miracle-working powers might not be diluted. She was only uncovered on her annual feast days and in times of extreme crisis when she

FIGURE 3. Giacomo Franco, *The Procession of Corpus Christi,* Plate XXV in Franco's *Habiti d'huomeni et donne venetiane con la processione della serenissima signoria et altri partico-lari cioè trionfi feste cerimonie publiche della nobilissima citta' di Venetia* (Venice, 160?). Photo credit: Art & Architecture Collection, Miriam and Ira D. Wallach Division of Art, Prints and Photographs, The New York Public Library, Astor, Lenox and Tilden Foundations.

would be brought in procession from the suburban village of Impruneta to Florence and displayed to a populace made desperate by plague, famine, or flood. The miracle-working image of the Santissima Annunziata in Florence was also normally kept under wraps, opened for viewing only on the day of the Annunciation.

Viewing sacred objects had such apparent salutary power that those anxious to maintain social order and to receive the benefits of the sacred frequently attempted to make the transitory effects of the religious procession permanent by creating a network of images that can be viewed in the streets throughout the city. On nearly every street corner in the back alleys of Venice, one can still find images of the Virgin. She usually presents herself as a modest statue or crude painting, or sometimes only a faded picture postcard tacked up within a niche or frame (*capitello*) on the outside wall of a house. Hundreds of images of Mary, the saints, and Christ proliferated throughout the city, encouraged by religious orders and parish priests but most often produced by neighborhood, family, or individual devotions. Beginning in 1450 the Venetian Senate charged a local patrician in each neighborhood with the responsibility for watching over these images, and in the residential neighborhoods the images still flourish.[13] How did contemporaries imagine these shrines worked? Why did they think that by merely making *visible* a sacred object or image the behavior of the populace could be improved?

The late medieval belief in the spiritual benefits derived from sighting the sacred has received considerable attention from scholars.[14] Richard Trexler's analysis of Giovanni Morelli's visionary experiences after spending hours staring fixedly at images of Christ and several saints reveals a psychological predisposition, even in a none-too-pious businessman in fifteenth-century Florence, to employ the gaze as a means for gaining access to his deeply troubling emotions.[15] Eamon Duffy demonstrates how the physical configurations of English churches were carefully planned to maximize the opportunities parishioners had to view the elevated Host through squints—peep holes placed in rood screens—and how the effect was multiplied by the priests who carefully sequenced the timing of masses on side altars so that one elevation followed another.[16] To understand fully this ubiquitous fascination with the visibility of the sacred, it is necessary to examine how contemporaries thought vision worked.

As a number of scholars have shown, the period from Al-Kindi to Kepler was one of tremendous intellectual ferment in optical theory among both theologians and students of optics in the arts faculties of medieval universities.[17] The debate rotated around two opposing theories: on the one hand, the Platonic theory of extromission, in which the eye is active and sends out luminous rays that act upon objects to produce sight, and on the other, the Aristotelian theory of intromission, in which the eye is passive and in the presence of light receives images conveyed through a transparent medium. By the beginning of the fourteenth century, variations on the Aristotelian theory dominated the debates. The Aristotelian dictum that nothing can be known about the material world unless first perceived by the senses led many thinkers to connect epistemology and the very foundations of semantics to optics. To know was to see. The problem was how do humans see? Despite William of Ockham's trenchant criticisms of the "perspectivists," as the followers of Roger Bacon were known to late medieval readers, Bacon's doctrine of the "multiplication of species" remained the central proposition in the standard theory of perception and cognition based on perception.

Katherine Tachau has noted how Bacon believed that psychological and mental processes could only be understood as manifestations of the physical processes of vision produced through the dissemination of light. Bacon's theory depended on the idea that all objects produce emanations, called "species" that multiply within a medium. These emanating species were variously described as rays or ripples, like the ripples produced in a pond after a stone is thrown in it. The species are projected outward and act on the eye creating sensations in the brain registered as images. For Bacon the visible species were a specific example of a general principle of the multiplication of species by all objects in the universe:

> Every efficient cause acts through its own power, which it exercises on the adjacent matter, as the light (*lux*) of the sun exercises its power on the air (which power is light [*lumen*] diffused through the whole world from the solar light [*lux*]). And this power is called 'likeness,' 'image,' and 'species,' and is designated by many other names, and it is produced both by substance and by accident, spiritual and corporeal ... this species produces every action in the world, for it acts on sense, on the intellect, and on all matter of the world for the generation of things.[18]

Species generate additional species in the medium contiguous to them, just as objects generate species of themselves in the medium of air, and these continuously multiplied species are projected along rays in all directions from all points on the object's surface until the rays meet obstructions. Once received by the eye, the species continue to multiply through the optic nerves to the brain. The enormous power of Bacon's conception of species can be seen in the startling range of synonyms he employs for them: "virtus, similitudo, ymago, ydolum, simulacrum, fantasma, forma, intentio, passio, impressio, and umbra philosophorum."[19]

Bacon's theory thus depends on the assumption that the emanations of objects through species are received by a viewer passively. Species leave a lasting impression on the senses, an impression transmitted to the brain as a "concept." The viewer, therefore, assimilates concepts rather than cogitates about them: insofar as species present exact likenesses of the generating objects, external reality is *re*-presented rather than represented in the mind.[20] According to the "radiation principle" of the optics of sight, seeing a sacred object is a way of making it *present* within the viewer, a way of employing a physical, sensory process to transmit spiritual influences.

There were, however, numerous difficulties in Bacon's theory that produced a thriving industry of commentators. For our purposes the central difficulty is the Baconian paradox of material species acting on the immaterial intellect, a paradox that raises the distinction between materiality and spirituality. The Franciscan theologian, Peter Olivi, proposed a critique of the Baconian theory that exposed the difficulties inherent in explaining spiritual influences through mechanical processes.

To Olivi the problem was that Bacon's notion of active species and passive cognition threatened free will. If species were material, Olivi argued, then they would operate upon the brain in a mechanical fashion, extending themselves through the optical nerve to create a mental concept of the object viewed, and the viewer would be utterly incapable of cogitating about or evaluating concepts received in this passive fashion. If, however, species were understood to be spiritual, then the problems created by corporeal species would be solved. The spiritual species would gain the soul's "virtual attention," because spiritual powers, understood as *virtutes,* would not act mechanically on the mind but in cooperation with the soul. From the Olivian position, there would be no distinction to be made between the normal operations of sight and a spiritual vision because both would operate according to the same laws of the *virtutes.* Seeing an object from the material world would be no different from seeing a sacred vision from God. The spiritual character of species created a unified theory of sight that did not distinguish between natural and supernatural visual experiences.

Whether one followed Bacon's perspectivist theory that posited the *material* emanations of species acting upon a passive viewer, Olivi's theory that treated the species as *spiritual* emanations that attracted the attention of the soul, or one of the many other variants, it is clear that the most common optical theories before Kepler emphasized how the very act of seeing an object brought the viewer under the influence of that object. Now here is the weak point in my argument: I certainly cannot show nor would I even imagine it to be true that the average lay viewer of a procession, if there were such a person, understood anything about these debates in optical theory. I cannot even show that the educated ecclesiastics and civic officials who organized processions always understood such matters. But these theories were widely disseminated, having extensively influenced, for example, the poets of late medieval love lyrics.[21] I can, moreover, show a pattern of behavior that implies a common understanding that viewing a sacred object or a sacred image brought the viewer under the influence of that image. This observation is confirmed by Lee Wandel's study of Ulrich Zwingli's iconoclasm: to the Protestant reformers the problem with images was not that they were impotent idols but that they emitted such powerful emanations they blocked out the ability of churchgoers to receive the Word of scripture as proclaimed by the reformist preachers.[22] The Protestant Reformation from this point of view can be understood as a revolution that attempted to privilege messages received through the ear over those that entered through the eye.

If this exposition of the radiation principle is correct, then the goal of the civic and church officials, pious groups, and individuals who displayed sacred images in late medieval and Renaissance Europe was to create numerous points for beneficent spiritual emanations that would project piety, passivity, and peacefulness into the souls of the populace. These emanation points could be created by street corner images, which would radiate over as much civic space as possible. Or they could be periodically reinvigorated through civic processions. Either way, the goal was to irradiate the population, to create multiple sources for salutary material or spiritual rays that would clog the mean streets of the city with a surfeit of piety. One of the differences, however, between street corner images and processions was obvious but telling. The procession included besides sacred objects, people, typically ecclesiastics or civic officials whose authority when so displayed also irradiated the city.

Now let me reverse the direction of the radiation of species by asking what did the people who walked in the procession see? This question is especially crucial in considering the ubiquitous processions of civic officials, princes, bishops, and popes. Certainly their exalted location in the procession gave them a privileged spot to absorb the beneficent rays of the sacred objects they carried and in some sense to influence the spectators merely by being seen. But as they walked they surveyed the urban scene and were, in effect, in the same position as the citizens of Siena who passed by the *Maestà,* except that they were surveying the spectators as well as being the objects of view. Through the operations of sight, they came under the influence of the spectators just as they sent out emanations toward those who looked at them. In processions the distinction between the seeing subject and the object viewed became blurred. If the species of sight were going in both directions, then the space around a procession must have been densely packed with powerful emanations.

The Matteo Pagan engraving of *The Procession of the Doge on Palm Sunday* (1556–59, fig. 4) employs a flattened perspective to recreate the visual experience of the procession, which cannot be grasped from a single point of view but demands eye movement and even the repositioning of the body to take in the entire scene because these engravings were originally produced in a series of large sheets that, put together, nearly covered an entire wall.[23] The linearity of the ducal procession as it passes through Piazza San Marco is paralleled by the line of female spectators arranged in the balconies of the Procuratoria Vecchia on the north side of the Piazza.

This rigid gender segregation of marching men and watching women positively cries out for an analysis of the gaze, which Bronwen Wilson has completed for this and other Venetian engravings from this period.[24] It is evident that the viewer and the object of the gaze here are entirely interchangeable. While the women may be gazing on the men who are decked out in their ceremonial robes of office and carrying symbolic objects of political authority, the processing officials can also be seen gazing at others.[25] They are gazing at one another, at those who view the engraving, and at the women in the balconies. Who is influencing whom here through the species of sight?

Many artists who represented processions considered the observers of processions as much a part of the visual scene as the procession itself. In figure 5, Gentile Bellini's *Miracle of the Holy Cross,* the women dressed in their jewels and lined up along the embankment convey a sense of iconic gravity that surpasses the icon itself, which had fallen from the bridge and has been rescued by a swimmer in the canal. The line of kneeling women have their eyes riveted on the miraculous cross held up by the swimming confraternity member in an intense field of interlinking visual species. The

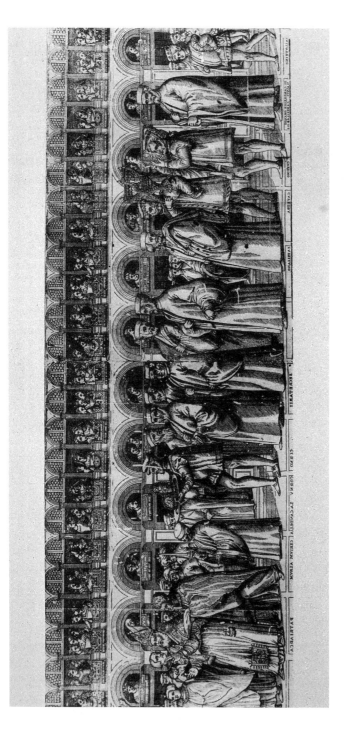

FIGURE 4. Matteo Pagan, *The Procession of the Doge on Palm Sunday* (1556–59). Photo credit: Museo Civico Correr, Venice.

FIGURE 5. Gentile Bellini, *Miracle of the Holy Cross* (1496–97). Accademia, Venice. Photo credit: Erich Lessing / Art Resource, NY.

radiations of the cross can be virtually traced across the visual space between the pious women on the left and the cross itself.

The sumptuous dress of the women in this and other representations of processions is not mere decoration. Gold, jewels, beautiful things, beautiful people do not just honor the sacred; they emit species worthy of being cast upon the sacred. Diane Owen Hughes's studies of sumptuary legislation and Renaissance understandings of the dangerous power of women's jewelry reveal a peculiar ambivalence in official legislation that attempted to regulate and limit the amount of jewelry women could own, but the very same officials who promulgated the restrictive legislation allowed, even demanded, that women display their jewelry when the city's honor was at stake.[26] The

women are the means through which the community exchanged sacred species for reverential ones. Kneeling women lining the streets became a fixture
in Renaissance processions. As specialists in the behavioral forms of submission and as living icons of beauty, spectating women were as necessary to
the procession as marching men. Their presence could even be employed
as a way of modifying the intent of a procession, as a way of transforming
a rite of submission into one of supplication. In 1507, for example, when
King Louis XII made a triumphal entry into Genoa after suppressing a rebellion against the occupying French forces, the Genoese citizens lined the
parade route with the "virgins" of Genoa, rows of young girls who knelt
before the triumphant conquering king and begged for mercy.[27] One might
suspect that the Genoese hoped that the emanations of innocence from
these girls would change the hard heart of King Louis even though Louis's
triumph was clearly intended to enforce submission.[28]

Although the fickleness of the human gaze produced a certain inter-
changability between the gazer and the gazed upon, processions still established social distinctions, and not just gendered ones. The very reciprocity
of the mutual gazes of interlocking material species, moreover, gave sub-
stance to the mutuality of social bonds among distinct social groups. What
the prince or civic officials saw as they processed created the ritual performance just as what was radiated from the procession itself did. To be a public
figure in the premodern period, whether a priest, bishop, pope, city coun-
cilor, prince, or king, was to be seen walking or riding in processions. To be
a disenfranchised woman, a layman, citizen, or subject was to watch those
who appeared in processions. If those who processed became public figures
by doing so, then those who as an anonymous collectivity watched them
became, in effect, the community, the *popolo* to put it in Italian terms. What
those who marched saw were the consequences of their public actions, and
thus good government would be mirrored in well-ordered civic spaces and
well-mannered citizens. Good government could be seen.

In Ambrogio Lorenzetti's *Allegory of the Good Government* (fig. 6) in the
Sala dei Nove in the Palazzo Pubblico in Siena, the genders are segregated as
in Pagan's engraving of the procession in Venice (fig. 4), in this case with the
female personifications of the virtues ranked above processing men. Randolph Starn and Loren Partridge have analyzed this gendering of Lorenzetti's
allegory.

FIGURE 6.   Ambrogio Lorenzetti, *Allegory of the Good Government* (1338–39), north wall. Palazzo Pubblico, Siena. Photo Credit: Scala / Art Resource, NY.

That the virtues are feminine follows from grammatical protocol for abstract nouns and a long iconographical tradition. Their location in the upper register of the picture corresponds to a conventional set of displacements whereby the exclusion of real women from political life enables them to be represented as icons of higher values. In effect, the bonding of men through their daughters, sisters, and wives is elevated into a communion of virtue, while female fertility is thematized in the proliferation of symbolic forms. The figures on either end of the virtues' bench are emblematic projections of the feminine in their own right. Peace reclines in a white gown, the contours of her body and her alluring pose bidding for desire .... The upright figure of Justice, stern executioner of desire unbounded, brandishes a sword over the severed head of a black-bearded man. Lacking a real court, the fraternity of republican citizens looks up here to a fictive court of women representing the principles supposedly uniting and superintending it. And yet, lest there be any doubt about male prerogatives, the feminine court is centered on the overbearing patriarchal figure in Sienese white and black.[29]

The twenty-four figures in a line on the lower left, which represent the assembled civic officials, form a double file procession, each man grasping a rope, which is woven from the cords (*corda* puns *Concordia*) that dangle from the scales of Justice and which passes through their hands into the hand of the personification of the Common Good. On the north wall seen here, the members of the procession are quite literally tied to an allegorization of Good Government, creating a graphic Mirror for Magistrates in which the painter Lorenzetti has invited the viewers, who would have habitually been the council members deliberating in the room, to identify with the male figures in the procession, and, of course, the councilors would have marched in processions such as this one several times a year, but especially at the inaugural of their term of office.

On the east wall Lorenzetti painted his visualization of the effects of good government (fig. 7). The wall has a remarkable capacity to visually pull the spectator into the scene despite its inconsistent perspective and multiple points of view. Jack M. Greenstein has suggested that the ideal vantage point is outside the fresco but within the room, specifically from the eyes of the reclining figure of Peace (fig. 6) as she gazes outside the visual frame of her wall to the east wall showing the effects of good government.

> Seen from an angle consistent with the gaze of Peace, the fresco takes on the characteristics of a true (by fourteenth-century standards) perspectival view. The buildings, which before had seemed askew, align themselves with the picture plane; the size of the figures diminishes in relation to their distance from the viewer (that is, Peace), not from an imaginary point within the picture; and, finally, instead of arbitrarily growing deeper as it approaches the south margin, the landscape ranges across concentric chains of hills until it reaches a horizon located at the farthest corner of the visual field.[30]

FIGURE 7. Ambrogio Lorenzetti, *Allegory of the Good Government: Effects of the Good Government on the City* (1338–39), east wall. Palazzo Pubblico, Siena. Photo Credit: Scala / Art Resource, NY.

From Greenstein's account, the scene is an illumination of a concept, an interpretation consistent with Baconian visual theories. However, given the inconsistencies of fourteenth-century perspective, it may be quixotic to establish too precisely the ideal vantage point. It could be located among the members of the civic procession as easily as with the reclining figure of Peace. If the figures of processing civic officials were, in some respect, the ideal viewers of the east wall (and their human counterparts were the actual viewers of the wall whenever they deliberated in the council chamber), the configuration of the fresco would have suggested to the Sienese officials what the city and countryside should look like when they marched in a procession if they followed the precepts of Good Government. The fresco provided a visual model for what officials would see in a procession, and the two walls illustrate the reflexivity of viewer and object, of what citizens would ideally see in the conduct of their elected officials on the north wall and what those officials would see were they to govern properly on the east.

Good government would, therefore, have visual effects. Buildings would be kept in good repair, commerce would thrive, students would study, and young women, made secure by the caress of good government, would be literally dancing in the streets. The moral implications of this visualization were clear to contemporaries. In 1427, Bernardino of Siena preached a sermon in the piazza just outside the Palazzo Pubblico and saw in the frescos in the Sala dei Nove a moral allegory (fig. 7):

> I see merchants buying and selling. I see dancing, the houses being repaired, the workers busy in the vineyards or sowing the fields, while on horseback others ride down to swim in the rivers; maidens I see going to a wedding, and great flocks of sheep and many another peaceful sight. Besides which I see a man hanging from the gallows, suspended there in the cause of justice. And for the sake of all these things men live in peace and harmony with one another.[31]

Bernardino, of course, was looking at a fresco, not a procession. The moral interpretation of actual processions eluded such allegorical fixity. Because of the kinesis of the procession and the instability of who was looking at whom, processions represent the ultimate failure of iconography to control meaning. The inability to control meaning is perhaps why organizers of processions were often so keen on attempting just that by decking them out with elaborate floats and mottos that explained to viewers what they were seeing. Processions had many meanings, perhaps as many meanings as observers, but I would suggest that one can come closer to understanding those meanings by examining how people behaved around the occasion of a procession rather than how they talked about it. Rituals employ sight in order to give access to emotional, psychological, or spiritual states that often resist expression in language, which is precisely the power of rituals and which is one of the reasons why the masters of logo-centrism, the humanists and Protestant reformers, so distrusted ritual, a term they invented

FIGURE 8.   Giacomo Franco, *Arsenal Sailors Carry the Doge-Elect, His Relatives, and the Admiral, Who Throw out Coins to the Crowd before the Coronation*, Plate XX in Franco's *Habiti d'huomeni et donne venetiane con la processione della serenissima signoria et altri particolari cioè trionfi feste cerimonie publiche della nobilissima citta' di Venetia* (Venice, 160?). Photo credit: Art & Architecture Collection, Miriam and Ira D. Wallach Division of Art, Prints and Photographs, The New York Public Library, Astor, Lenox and Tilden Foundations.

during the sixteenth century to describe a vain, meaningless activity. Ritual to them was textless, or spun out multiple texts, or mutilated the official text of interpretation, or worst of all, muddled the meaning of God's Word. As Ernst Cassirer put it, to engage in a ritual experience is to live "a life of emotion, not of thoughts."[32]

Crowds were often not as passive in watching processions as the previous examples might suggest. The frenzied response of the crowd to the procession to present the newly elected doge of Venice suggests the distinctive reflexivity of processions exhibited through behavior (fig. 8). The Venetian spectators were looking for and scrambling after the coins the new doge and his relatives threw out from a float carried by arsenal sailors. This vestige of the ancient right of the people to the "ritual pillage" of the goods of a new prince or king literally acted out the optical theory of emanations.[33] The metallic emanations of coins supplanted the spiritual species of the liturgical procession, creating a sensational response among the spectators. The comparison here between the emanations of optical species and the distribution of coins is, of course, contrived, but it illustrates precisely what I think is always going on in a procession—an intense exchange of visual and affective influences between the procession and its spectators. Here coins were exchanged for homage. In the liturgical procession spiritual power was exchanged for expressions of piety. The processors owed something of value to the spectators who in return offered deference, whether deference to political authorities or to God.

As the example of Bruegel's *The Fight between Carnival and Lent* (fig. 1) illustrates with its profusion of responses that contrasted between the ribald and the reverent, processions evoked strong emotional reactions in those who viewed and participated in them. Although one could trace the iconographical significations in the painting, those identifiable meanings hardly account for the dynamism of the emotions displayed in the painting. Something seems to be operating that is independent of hermeneutics, something that is liberated from the fixity of a text and its potential interpretations. The instability of meaning in rituals is not just a symptom of postmodernist theoretical angst but the very source of creative tension in rituals that Bruegel seems to have recognized. Processions either activate emotions in spectators—emotions of piety or anger, patriotic enthusiasm or rebellion— or they are terribly boring, the big yawn of a Rose Bowl Parade on television. Then they had become "mere rituals" because no matter what people saw, they missed the emanations.

NOTES

I wish to dedicate this essay to the memory of the late Bob Scribner, whose studies on ritual and ways of seeing have deeply influenced my own work. In particular, see his "Ways of Seeing in the Age of Dürer," in *Dürer and His Culture,* ed. Dagmar Eichbergern and Charles Zika (Cambridge, 1998), 93–117.

1. On the cultural motif of the battle between Carnival and Lent, see Peter Burke, *Popular Culture in Early Modern Europe* (New York, 1978), 178–243.

2. On the iconographic interpretation, see C. G. Stridbeck, "'The Combat of Carnival and Lent' by Pieter Bruegel the Elder: An Allegorical Picture of the Sixteenth Century," *Journal of the Warburg and Courtauld Institutes* 19 (1956): 96–109; Claude Gaignebet, "Le combat de Carnaval et de Carême de P. Breugel (1559)," *Annales: Économies, Sociétés, Civilizations* 27 (1972): 313–47; and idem, *Le Carnaval* (Paris, 1974). Cf. Martine Grinberg, "Les combats de Carnaval et de Carême: Trajets d'une métaphore," *Annales: Économies, Sociétés, Civilizations* 38 (1983): 65–98.

3. On the violent potential of ritual performances, see the classic essays by Natalie Zemon Davis, "The Reasons of Misrule" and "The Rites of Violence," in *Society and Culture in Early Modern France* (Stanford, CA, 1975), 97–123 and 152–87 respectively.

4. On invented traditions, see *Rituals of Royalty: Power and Ceremonial in Traditional Societies,* ed. David Cannadine and Simon Price (Cambridge, 1987). On the attempts to codify rituals, see Richard C. Trexler, *The Libro Cerimoniale of the Florentine Republic* (Geneva, 1978).

5. Edward Muir, *Ritual in Early Modern Europe,* 1st ed. (Cambridge, 1997; 2nd ed., 2005), chapter 5.

6. Arnold van Gennep, *The Rites of Passage,* trans. Monika B. Vizedom and Gabrielle L. Caffee (Chicago, 1960).

7. Cf. Philippe Buc, *The Dangers of Ritual: Between Early Medieval Texts and Social Scientific Theory* (Princeton, NJ, 2001), which argues texts are about texts and not about actual ritual events, and therefore the entire endeavor to recapture ritual events from the past should be abandoned. For the most sophisticated analysis of how ritual actions must be distinguished from intentions and prescribed meanings, see Caroline Humphrey and James Laidlaw, *The Archetypal Actions of Ritual: A Theory of Ritual Illustrated by the Jain Rite of Worship* (Oxford, 1994).

8. My claim that the most important object usually appeared in the center of the procession is based upon reading numerous books of ceremonies, for example, Archivio di Stato, Venice (ASV), Collegio Cerimoniale 1; ASV, Regina Margherita, B-14, series LXXCI, no. 6; and Trexler, *The Libro Cerimoniale.* For a theoretical discussion of the same principle, see Clifford Geertz, "Centers, Kings, and Charisma: Reflections on the Symbolics of Power," in *Culture and Its Creators: Essays in Honor of Edward Shils,* ed. Joseph Ben-David and Terry Nichols Clark (Chicago, 1977), 150–71.

9. Peter Brown, *The Cult of the Saints: Its Rise and Function in Latin Christianity* (Chicago, 1981). For a similar argument about Renaissance rituals, see Richard C. Trexler, *Public Life in Renaissance Florence* (New York, 1980), 47–54.

10. Craig M. Koslofsky, *The Reformation of the Dead: Death and Ritual in Early Modern Germany, 1450–1700* (New York, 2000). Cf. Susan C. Karant-Nunn, *The Reformation of Ritual: An Interpretation of Early Modern Germany* (London and New York, 1997).

11. Bram Kempers, "Icons, Altarpieces, and Civic Ritual in Siena Cathedral, 1100–1530," in *City and Spectacle in Medieval Europe*, ed. Barbara A. Hanawalt and Kathryn L. Reyerson (Minneapolis, 1994), 89–136, and Diana Norman, *Siena and the Virgin: Art and Politics in a Late Medieval City State* (New Haven and London, 1999), 1–3.

12. Richard C. Trexler, "Florentine Religious Experience: The Sacred Image," *Studies in the Renaissance* 19 (1972): 7–41.

13. Edward Muir, "The Virgin on the Street Corner: The Place of the Sacred in Italian Cities," in *Religion and Culture in the Renaissance and Reformation*, ed. Steven Ozment (Kirksville, MO, 1989), 25–42. On earlier examples of the place of the sacred, see Augustine Thompson, *Cities of God: The Religion of the Italian Communes, 1125–1325* (University Park, PA, 2005).

14. The most influential work in this vein is David Freedberg, *The Power of Images: Studies in the History and Theory of Response* (Chicago and London, 1989).

15. Trexler, *Public Life in Renaissance Florence*, 159–86.

16. Eamon Duffy, *The Stripping of the Altars: Traditional Religion in England, 1400–c. 1580* (New Haven, CT, 1992).

17. David C. Lindberg, *Theories of Vision from Al-Kindi to Kepler* (Chicago, 1976); idem, "The Science of Optics" in *Science in the Middle Ages*, ed. David Lindberg (Chicago, 1978), 338–68; Katherine H. Tachau, *Vision and Certitude in the Age of Ockham: Optics, Epistemology and the Foundations of Semantics* (Leiden, 1988); A. C. Crombie, *Science, Optics and Music in Medieval and Early Modern Thought* (London, 1990); and David Allen Park, *The Fire within the Eye: A Historical Essay on the Nature and Meaning of Light* (Princeton, NJ, 1997). On the application of these theories to painting, see Graziella Federici Vescovini, *Studi sulla prospettiva medievale* (Turin, 1965).

18. Quoted in Tachau, *Vision and Certitude in the Age of Ockham*, 7–8.

19. Ibid, 8n.

20. Cf. Freedberg, *The Power of Images*, 27–40.

21. Dana E. Stewart, *The Arrow of Love: Optics, Gender, and Subjectivity in Medieval Love Poetry* (Lewisburg, PA, 2003).

22. Lee Palmer Wandel, "The Reform of the Images: New Visualizations of the Christian Community at Zürich," *Archiv für Reformationsgeschichte* 80 (1989): 105–24 and idem, *Voracious Idols and Violent Hands: Iconoclasm in Reformation Zurich, Strasbourg, and Basel* (Cambridge, 1995).

23. On the Pagan engraving, see Jeffrey Kurtzman and Linda Maria Koldau, "*Trombe, Trombe d'argento, Trombe squarciate, Tromboni,* and *Piffari* in Venetian Processions and Ceremonies of the Sixteenth Century," *Journal of Seventeenth-Century Music* 8 (2002); Iain Fenlon, "Music, Ceremony and Self-Identity in Renaissance Venice," *Music & Anthropology* 1 (1996); idem, "Magnificence as Civic Image: Music and Ceremonial Space in Early Modern Venice," in *Music and Musicians in Renaissance Cities and Towns*, ed. Fiona Kisby (Cambridge, 2001), 28–44.

24. Bronwen Moira Siobhan Wilson, *The World in Venice: Print, the City, and Early Modern Identity* (Toronto, 2005).

25. These symbolic objects were known as the *trionfi,* which borrowed from the sacrality of relics by their prominent placement in the procession. See Edward Muir, *Civic Ritual in Renaissance Venice* (Princeton, NJ, 1981), 103–19 and *passim.*

26. Diane Owen Hughes, "Sumptuary Law and Social Relations in Renaissance Italy," in *Disputes and Settlements: Law and Human Relations in the West,* ed. John Bossy (Cambridge, 1983), 69–99; idem, "Representing the Family: Portraits and Purposes in Early Modern Italy," *Journal of Interdisciplinary History* 17 (1986): 7–38; and idem, "Distinguishing Signs: Ear-Rings, Jews and Franciscan Rhetoric in the Italian Renaissance City," *Past and Present* 112 (1986): 3–59.

27. George L. Gorse, "Between Empire and Republic: Triumphal Entries into Genoa during the Sixteenth Century," in *"All The World's a Stage . . .": Art and Pageantry in the Renaissance and Baroque,* ed. Barbara Wisch and Susan Scott Munshower (University Park, PA, 1990), 188–257.

28. There is a vast literature on entries. One of the best studies is Peter Arnade, *Realms of Ritual: Burgundian Ceremony and Civic Life in Late Medieval Ghent* (Ithaca and London, 1996).

29. Randolph Starn and Loren Partridge, *Arts of Power: Three Halls of State in Italy, 1300–1600* (Berkeley, 1992), 51; and Randolph Starn, *Ambrogio Lorenzetti: The Palazzo Pubblico, Siena* (New York, 1994).

29. Starn and Partridge, *Arts of Power,* 49.

30. Jack M. Greenstein, "The Vision of Peace: Meaning and Representaion in Ambrogio Lorenzetti's Sala della Pace Cityscapes," *Art History* 11 (1988): 497.

31. Quoted in Starn and Partridge, *Arts of Power,* 46.

32. Ernst Cassirer, *The Myth of the State* (New Haven, CT, 1946), 24.

33. On ritual pillages, see Laurie Nussdorfer, "The Vacant See: Ritual and Protest in Early Modern Rome," *Sixteenth Century Journal* 18 (1987): 173–89; Carlo Ginzburg, coordinator of the Bologna seminar, "Ritual Pillages: A Preface to Research in Progress," in *Microhistory and the Lost Peoples of Europe,* ed. Edward Muir and Guido Ruggiero (Baltimore, 1991), 20–41; and Joëlle Rollo-Koster, "Looting the Empty See: The Great Western Schism Revisited (1378)," *Rivista storia della Chiesa in Italia* 59 (2005): 429–74.

Index

Page numbers in italics refer to figures.